THE FOUNDATION OF THIS BOOK SERIES IS BASED
OFF THESE TWO SCRIPTURES.

The heavens are the heavens of the Lord,
But the earth He has given to the sons
of men. Psalm 115:16 NASB

For our struggle is not against flesh and blood
[contending only with physical opponents], but
against the rulers, against the powers, against the
world forces of this [present] darkness, against
the spiritual forces of wickedness in the heavenly
(supernatural) places. Ephesians 6:12 Amplified

My expanded version of Ephesians 6:12 says
this: For our wrestling match is not against flesh
and blood [contending only with physical op-
ponents], not against persons with bodies, but
against cosmic powers or fallen angels within
four levels of the celestial realm who rule in var-
ious areas and in descending orders of authority.
Against world dominators of this present evil
age, and against spiritual forces of wickedness
in the heavenlies who have tiered authority.

EXPLORING SECRETS
OF THE
HEAVENLY REALMS

BRUCE HINES
WITH LEAH HINES

Contents

FOREWORD

After watching Bruce write this first book in about three months, I was initially overtaken at how quickly it all came about. As I read through the book, I can vividly remember the time frame of each story and each experience. I remember his first encounters with the fallen when God would send them down to be judged, because we encountered them together. I was there when he received a prophecy from one of our National prophets about how God would make known to Bruce the structure of the kingdom of darkness.

Because of the vast knowledge that God planned to share with Bruce, I watched and continue to watch, as the Lord drives Bruce to understand each spiritual experience through study, research and cause him to seek counsel by contacting every person he could find who had a true understanding about the fallen. Those specifically who had encountered them and who knew of them in the scriptures. I've watched his integrity as he studied to show himself approved before teaching the members of our church and ministry about the fallen. It was seven years after his first encounter before he spoke publicly about the fallen. Even though this book he wrote this book in three months; It took over 20 years of combined study and the fruits of experience through healing and deliverance ministry.

Over the years, we have prayed for thousands of people suffering from spiritual and emotional wounds, mental issues, and demonic complications all the while rejoicing with them in their healing. As we understood the structure of the fallen, we rejoiced with families as they were being reconciled and healed after God judged the fallen over the family lines.

If everyone would read and understand "Exploring Secrets of the Heavenly Realms" series, churches, the people in them and their families, our cities, our nations and even our world would change. In Acts 28:27 Luke reminds us of what the prophet Isaiah said in Isaiah 6:9, 10. I pray that you will have the heart to understand, the ears to hear, the eyes to know and be acquainted with the mysteries of the heavenly realms. As you read the rest of this book, you will understand the difference between demons and the fallen.

Leah Ann Hines

Co-Founder and Co-Pastor
Church in One Accord
www.churchinoneaccord.org

INTRODUCTION

This book was an unplanned book. My wife and I were talking, and I was explaining to her that I was ready for a break in my writing but there was at least one more book of "Exploring Secrets of the Heavenly Realms" series in me. I was describing to her, I would call the future book "The Coming War." Immediately she hit the floor and started to groan and travail, then the Holy Spirit spoke to her a few words, "It Is Written." Travail quit when I said, "Jesus I accept the assignment."

The higher we go in the heavenly realms, the more accountable the person becomes. The word tempted means to be tested or evaluated, to be approved or disapproved. When the devil came to test Jesus, he said, "it is written."

When we engage in fallen angel deliverance, the definition means to come or to approach with a request. Jesus was tested in the wilderness as the tempter came with proposals, suggestions, or questions as the definition states. When we make the words of our mouths agree with the Word of God, we position ourselves to receive the full backing and authority of Jesus.

There are two laws that seem to override sin, rebellion, and evil. These laws are, "it is written," quoting scripture and the second, the laws of prayer. These two laws combined have taken out some of the highest ranking fallen angels over churches and family bloodlines. The laws of prayer and quoting the scriptures are the two highest laws of the universe.

God has called us to a wrestling match. Simply put, our wrestling match is with the nature of the fallen angels, sin! Moses says there are the hosts of heaven or the heavenly bodies filled with the vast multitude of different angels set up as a military army with campaign-like operations intended to achieve certain objectives. They seek the goal of these objectives through a multi-level army campaign that is offensive in nature through different maneuvers and strategies, individually, organizationally, territorially and globally.

The Bible defines a spoken declaration as aggressive; It is a word of spiritual warfare. When we declare, it is releasing the authority and power of God's Word into the earth. This affects our life, the life of the Church, and the universe. The greatest and most effective way to release the power of God into a situation is to declare God's Word. It is our job as heralds to go out into our cities with a declaration concerning the will and decisions of God. We are to decree to the rulers and authorities over our cities the will and decisions of God. We are to announce God's will and to pray His decisions into existence. We are to call those things that are not as though they are in prayer.

We are to watch our words carefully, remembering how Jesus defeated the devil in the wilderness and how Michael the archangel spoke to the devil. In each case, the Word of God or the Father Himself spoke. Jesus quoted the written

Word. Michael asks God for a rebuke. The promise is that if we speak properly, we will have very little trouble with the fallen angels when God sends them down for judgment.

Today the local church must set a pattern of activities that brings the power of the Holy Spirit. It all starts with prayer and worship. Then we must teach a gospel of power. I love to teach doctrine and theology, but it will always be proclaimed as having power.

In this book series, we have learned that Satan delegates high-ranking members of the hierarchy of fallen angels to control nations, regions, cities, tribes, people groups, neighborhoods, and other significant social networks of human beings worldwide.

I hope the reader enjoys the powerful truths that are about to be revealed in this book. I encourage everyone to buy the series, so they would be up to date on the coming move of the Church at the close of this evil age.

Bruce Hines

Author and Sr. Pastor
Church in One Accord

I hope you have enjoyed the book series "Exploring Secrets of the Heavenly Realms" and that you will write a favorable review on Amazon.

PART ONE

~

IT IS WRITTEN
BRUCE HINES

CHAPTER ONE

PROCLAIMING SPIRITUAL AUTHORITY

There are words that seem to bring spiritual power when they are spoken. Jesus shows us this truth through a power encounter with the highest of fallen archangels, the ruler of the kingdom of darkness, Satan.

Then Jesus was led up by the Spirit into the wilderness to be tempted by the devil. And after He had fasted forty days and forty nights, He then became hungry. And the tempter came and said to Him, "If You are the Son of God, command that these stones become bread." But He answered and said, "It is written, 'Man shall not live on bread alone, but on every word that proceeds out of the mouth of God.'" Then the devil took Him into the

holy city and had Him stand on the pinnacle of
the temple, and *said to Him, "If You are the Son
of God, throw Yourself down; for it is written, 'He
will command His angels concerning You'; and
'On their hands they will bear You up, So that
You will not strike Your foot against a stone.'"
Jesus said to him, "On the other hand, it is writ-
ten, 'You shall not put the Lord your God to the
test.'" Again, the devil took Him to a very high
mountain and showed Him all the kingdoms of
the world and their glory; and he said to Him,
"All these things I will give You, if You fall down
and worship me." Then Jesus *said to him, "Go,
Satan! For it is written, 'You shall worship the
Lord your God, and [d]serve Him only.'" Then
the devil left Him; and behold, angels came and
began to minister to Him. Matthew 4:1-11 NASB

The Holy Spirit led Jesus into the wilderness. The word "led" means to lead up, lead, or bring into a higher place. Before Jesus' baptism and the Holy Spirit coming upon Him, He lived from the terrestrial or the earthly realm. Now the Holy Spirit was taking Jesus into the celestial realm or the second and third heaven. Notice, Jesus went out into the desert, but Satan had come down to the terrestrial realm to test Jesus concerning the things in the celestial realms. This is so clear when I am doing second heaven or fallen angel deliverance. The laws of the terrestrial realm differ completely from the celestial realm. The fallen angel God is judging will obey the minister if that minister is operating from the heavenly realms. There are two things we must notice in the scriptures below: the levels of the courts and what the offense is.

> *"You have heard that the ancients were told, 'You shall not commit murder' and 'Whoever commits murder shall be liable to the court.' 22 But I say to you that everyone who is angry with his brother shall be guilty before the court; and whoever says to his brother, 'You good-for-nothing,' shall be guilty before the supreme court; and whoever says, 'You fool,' shall be guilty enough to go into the fiery hell. Matthew 5:21-22 NASB*

The higher we go in the heavenly realms, the more accountable the person becomes. The word tempted means to be tested or evaluated, to be approved or disapproved. This, too, I find in second heaven or fallen angel deliverance. The fallen angel being judged, depending on class and rank, will put the deliverance minister through a series of tests, waiting for the minister to say something illegal in the realm they are operating in. This is so clearly seen in Jesus' power encounter at the highest level.

This all explains the title of this book! When the devil came to test Jesus, he said! This is so common in second heaven deliverance of fallen angels. First, they will hardly say anything, looking at us in disgust and hate that we reflect God. When they first speak, it will more likely be a test. The fallen do this through the twisting of God's Word like the devil was doing to Jesus. The fallen angels will also accuse mankind of their sin nature and guilt. However,

Jesus ignored all the sayings of the devil and said, "it is written." These are words of notification, informing or announcing the process of God's laws and or His administration. When the believer speaks the Words of God, the scriptures, we are proclaiming the principles of divine reason and creative order. We are also proclaiming the principles of divine judgment.

The word proclaim is a strong word. It comes from a Latin word that means "to shout forth." A related word in the language of the New Testament is one that means "to confess." Confess means "to say the same as." For us, as believers in the Bible, confession involves saying the same thing with our mouths as God has already said in His Word. This is how Jesus, the Son of God, equal in the Trinity, answered the devil.

When the fallen angel engages in the deliverance, the definition means to come or to approach with a request. In verse three of Matthew 4, the tempter came with proposals, suggestions, or questions as the definition states. The believer must listen to the temptation or the accusation but respond with the Word of God. This requires hearing God and obeying the unction to quote scripture. The definition also speaks of coming forward or coming to engage or address.

When we make the words of our mouths agree with the Word of God, we position ourselves to receive the full backing and authority of Jesus. Then the kingdom of darkness in God's courtroom stands accused of crimes against

CHAPTER ONE

God and His Word.

Hebrews 3:1 states, "Therefore, holy brethren, partakers of a heavenly calling, consider Jesus, the Apostle and High Priest of our confession." The word "Apostle" comes from the word envoy, which comes from the word communicator, and the root word is master. Jesus is the master communicator and go-between or an envoy. Jesus came as God's representative to represent the interests of God. There is another definition used: it is a messenger, a heavenly being or angel as the definition states, who is on a mission. Therefore, we can conclude that angels, whether good or evil, are messengers with a mission. Here's my point: Jesus is God's messenger with a message and a mission. He was opposed by the kingdom of darkness' messenger with his mission. Both realms are engaged in a message!

The devil used a powerful word in the suggestion or temptation of Jesus in Matthew 4:3, that word was, command. This is where I got the title for this chapter. Command means to give instruction or to order. Command is to speak or talk, with an apparent focus upon the content of what is said and it comes from the root word ask. This is exactly what the fallen do where the demonic does not have the authority to say or to speak. The demonic will lie or threaten, but they do not have the authority to speak or to order. God never commissioned the demonic with positions of authority and responsibility. The fallen angels were at one time commissioned by God. The fallen were given tasks, with a mission or assignment, and it was their duty and responsibility to carry out that mission. They were given jurisdictional rights and were charged by God with those rights. What I am driving at is, they function in the same way they were created, levels of commissioning, jurisdictions of authority and mission assignments.

Therefore, Paul called the fallen angels the gods of this evil age and world dominators. They speak from realms of authority and God's Church must be fully trained and respect the fallen's authority. It is the church's job to find out their mission assignment; the jurisdiction and commission they operate in. We are to speak the power of God's written word against the fallen's assignments in a prayerful reminder to God. It is an awesome supernatural experience to say humbly, "it is written" to a fallen angel. I then watch the power of God move on the fallen in judgment.

Once we have covered their assignments, then it is time to bring out the eternal chains of darkness and prayerfully ask God to assign them to the pits of darkness or tartaros. God pronounces powerful words to the fallen for what they have done as in Psalm eighty-two. God said, you are gods [since you judge on My behalf, as My representatives]; indeed, all of you are children of the Most High, but you shall die as men and fall as one of the princes. To fall as one of the princes is to fall like mankind and to die for it. The judgement against the fallen is because they have violated their purpose and mission to which God called them.

Whenever we say with our mouths what the Bible says about us as believers in Christ, then we have Jesus as our High Priest in heaven, releasing His authority and His blessing over our confession. This spiritual principle is important when we are dealing with fallen angels. When we confess what the Word of God says, the fallen release family bloodlines. Therefore, we must ask God to send down the fallen angels over family bloodlines and have them confess their release of the family.

A declaration is a confession aggressively made. It is a word that speaks of spiritual warfare. It is releasing the authority of God's Word into a situation, into your own life, your family, the life of your church, a political situation, or whatever it may be. There are countless situations that need to have the power of God released into them, and there is no more effective way to release the power of God than by declaration.

The Hebrew definition for charge is to give an order or to command. Therefore, it is to charge someone to do something. To charge or to command is to give instructions to or direct somebody to do something with authority. This is what the believer is doing in a fallen angel deliverance. We are to speak the Word of God in prayer or in combat, depending on the fallen angels rank and jurisdictional authority. There seems to be a lot of grace with direct combat over family bloodlines than over territories.

Territorial fallen angel rights require prayer, and this is what Jesus meant when He said, "this kind only comes out by prayer and fasting" (Mark 9:29). The Greek word meaning for "kind" is a category of things distinguished by some common characteristic or quality. The Strong's defines it as "kin" and relates it to a family member. The Hebrew definition states an entity in contrast or different to other entities. J. P. Louw and E. A. Nida defines as a kind or type of entity, implying a contrast-comparison to other similar entities—'kind, type.' The definition explains that a kind or category is that of a class of entities. A class based upon an implied lineage and possessing certain derived characteristics; every kind of, or all sorts of.

Matthew 17 and Mark 9

Simply, Jesus is talking about fallen angels, not demons. The fallen angels fathered the demonic, and each shared common characteristics and quality (evil/sin). As each fallen angel has a dimension (throne, dominion, principality, power) or quality; a state of grade or superiority (rank) and caliber or capability of skills, so does the demonic have these characteristics. The demonic are kin or offspring and are of the family of the fallen angels. The definition plainly states that the fallen angels are different entities, evil angels, not hybrids of the human and fallen angel mixture. Jesus says that the disciples ran into a different class of evil, possessing different attributes and supernatural power.

In the Mark nine account, I am sure the reader picked up on all the demonic spirits in operation under deaf and dumb, which is a root spirit in the Bible. Jesus clues us in on something so much deeper, a lunatic (moonstruck) spirit. This spirit would come or approach the boy and seize or take a hold of him forcibly as if he were captured. A few pages ago I mentioned, when the fallen angel engages, the definition means to come or to approach with a request. The definition also speaks of coming forward or coming to engage or to address. The disciple did not know how to address or engage the fallen angel here! We know the spirit was fallen because of what Jesus says, "This kind only comes out by prayer and or fasting."

The King James Bible uses a powerful word, "teareth" him or the fallen angel comes to break, wreck or crack the soul by separation of parts, shattering into fragments of the mind, will and emotions. The fallen angel would order the lunatic or epileptic spirit to seize and shatter into alter personalities. The manifestation is the seizure and the foaming of the mouth. The Bible says from Jesus's words the devil is used as a metaphor for fallen angels, the divine power, deity, divinity (elohim); evil spirits or the messengers and ministers of the devil as the definition states.

How did Jesus handle the situation? He first noticed the kind behind it all, a fallen angel over the family bloodline. Secondly, He approached or came close to engage. Thirdly, He rebuked. To rebuke is to speak sharply of disapproving behavior and or actions. That translates back to what we have been talking about, finding out the assignment of the fallen angel and the demons at work.

Jesus deals with the fallen angel and all the demons come out. This, too, I see in a fallen angel deliverance. When I deal with the one in charge, those who are under his command and receiving orders are all driven out when their leader goes. Remember, we are talking about the power of speaking what God has declared in His Word. Just a few pages ago, we said that a charge is to command or to give instructions to or direct somebody to do something with authority. Instructions are plural and so Jesus went through a series of rebukes until the fallen angels assignments were stripped away. This is the pattern of over one thousand fallen angel deliverances. We do not leave it to, "What is God showing you or saying to you?", but directly confront as the disciples did, and as Jesus did.

TEACH AND PROCLAIM

When we look at the first four verses of Acts we read:

The first account I made, Theophilus, was [a continuous report] about all the things that Jesus began to do and to teach until the day when He ascended to heaven, after He had by the Holy Spirit given instruction to the apostles (special messengers) whom He had chosen. To these [men] He also showed Himself alive after His suffering [in Gethsemane and on the cross], by [a series of] many infallible proofs and unquestionable demonstrations, appearing to them over a period of forty days and talking to them about the things concerning the kingdom of God. While being together and eating with them, He commanded them not to leave Jerusalem, but to wait for what the Father had promised, "Of which," He said, "you have heard Me speak. Acts 1:1-4 Amplified

As we just read in the Matthew and Mark account, Jesus preached or publicly announced kingdom truths and principles while urging acceptance and compliance to His message. He taught to impart skills and knowledge concerning the kingdom of God that would change the course of this evil age. It is the job of Bible teachers to take part in the supernatural in such a way that the Word of God imparts supernatural skills and methods that transform the way the world sees the Church. In the Matthew seventeen and the Mark nine account, it was one of my first scriptures I found that began the unfolding of the second heaven and fallen angels.

Jesus continued to give instructions and to teach until the forty days were up and in just ten short days, the Holy Spirit would come and continue the teaching and the instructing. Jesus began or started to take the first steps in carrying out an action that would bring God's Kingdom to earth. When the Holy Spirit came at Pentecost, He continued to initiate a process that would introduce the Apostles to particular activities and skills that would change the course of this evil age. We have lost a lot of those mysteries the early Church walked in, but now the Holy Spirit is bringing back those secret truths.

Proclaiming is really the activity of a herald. Herald is a word we don't use very much today, but in medieval times, the herald was a person with authority from a king, a duke, or some other nobleman who would go to a public place and make a proclamation of the will and decision of that ruler. He would shout out, "Oyez, Oyez!" and then make the proclamation. So, whenever people heard "Oyez, Oyez," they knew it represented the voice of authority. They would stand at attention and listen to what was being said. In the New Testament, although it doesn't clearly come out in most translations, the word preach is the word for a herald. It means "to proclaim."

The Dictionary of Biblical Theology says, "Proclaim" is complementary to the more specific term "evangelize" (euangelizomai) or the phrase "announce the good news," which contains within its meaning the object that is announced or proclaimed—the good news. However, usually when "proclaim" (kērysso) is used the context includes its object, which in the majority of instances is the gospel or Jesus. The noun proclaimer, herald (kēryx), refers to one who proclaims news publicly. The teaching, instructions, and supernatural training that the disciples received from Jesus now the Holy Spirit would come to empower and impart. The disciples are now the Apostles, and with boldness they would proclaim the gospel.

Spiritual Authority

There are many ministries that preach the gospel, yet the fallen angels are not afraid of their preaching or the Word of God. Fallen angels are very much afraid of our being subject to the authority of the Word of God and how to manifests its power.

For the kingdom of God does not consist in words but in power. 1 Corinthians 4:20 NASB

God has called the Church to move in power that influences righteousness. This looses mankind from evil and binds the powers of darkness from their work. Yet most churches don't know the power and authority that it takes to transform regions from darkness to light, because they are untrained in spiritual warfare. It is the believer's lack of understanding of spiritual warfare that keeps regions bound in darkness. We know that the power of the Kingdom of God is righteousness, yet most don't see that the power of the Kingdom of Darkness is sin.

Spiritual authority is such a big subject. Without proper training and practical experience, there has been a lot of unnecessary information printed. Wisdom is the capacity to understand and as a result, to act wisely and in power. So operating in authority, we must understand the rules of engagement in the realm we desire to operate in and act wisely in exercising that power. Authority is the right to use power, but for power to have an effect or to succeed, it must be used correctly. Therefore, we must be fully trained. Someone who has been properly trained in authority will exhibit signs of power.

There is a conflict between the Kingdom of God and the Kingdom of Satan for the right to control the universe or the creation. This conflict is centered on who will have the authority. Our victory in the conflict with Satan and the fallen angels directly results from the ability to manifest that authority God has given us in Christ Jesus.

God has placed a great demand on mankind and that demand is to obey and fulfill the great commission. If the Church refuses to get involved in exercising spiritual authority over the kingdom of darkness, the world will be increasingly undermined and all authority will be overthrown and lawlessness will rule.

Have you ever thought how the fallen angels laugh when a rebellious person preaches the gospel, but does not heal the sick or cast out demons: or when an assembly refuses to fulfill the great commission through power ministry?

Chapter Two

Prayer and Spiritual Warfare

The reason we don't see the world accepting the gospel, turning to the Church, and God for answers is the lack of spiritual power against the kingdom of darkness.

And even if our gospel is veiled, it is veiled to those who are perishing, in whose case the god of this world has blinded the minds of the unbelieving so that they might not see the light of the gospel of the glory of Christ, who is the image of God. 2 Corinthians 4:3-4 NASB

A function of the Church is to impart skills and knowledge concerning the operations of the kingdom of darkness. If we do not understand how God operates, would it not also be true regarding the kingdom of darkness? During the times of Jesus, His teachings would astonish the crowds. The Greek word astonished is a strong word and could also be translated amazed or astounded. It also has a meaning: "to strike out, expel by a blow, drive out or away, to strike one out of self-possession". Jesus was explaining how the Kingdom of God has come to invade this evil age with authority and power, to bring redemption to all mankind and deliverance from demonic spirits and fallen angels.

Jesus' powerful message caused demons and evil spirits to be revealed. When Jesus preached, demonic activity revealed itself, and we see Jesus asserting His authority by casting it out. What an impact Jesus made, teaching about God's saving grace in himself, and authority over evil spirits and sickness. He imparted knowledge and skills to overcome this evil age empowered by sin. This is how the fallen angels are weakened in territories.

You may have read books on how prophetic intercessors wrestle with principalities and powers as Paul describes in Ephesians 6. The Ephesians 6:12 scripture is not only a prayer model but an action plan to stand against the schemes of the fallen angels. God has empowered the Church to stand against the devil's schemes. The schemes are the thoughts of our mind and its purpose through the craftiness of the fallen angels.

The spiritual cosmic nature of the opposition in the universe makes the armor of God absolutely necessary. This is the only place in the Pauline writings where believers are explicitly said to be in a battle against evil fallen powers in the second heaven. Paul lists the four dimensions of the second heaven in Colossians One but does not give clear warfare instructions.

In the late 1990s and early 2000s, Church began to raise up an international army to combat the enemy in the heavenly realms through prayer. The question is, was it really God? There were notable changes in the spiritual atmosphere in many places, but it was God's sovereign grace that allowed it. If it was God's perfect will, it would have remained. Why did it stop? Could it be the idea or the truth was correct, but the process was wrong?

Some authors imply influential leaders became fearful that such warfare might involve casualties of war, and these leaders began to share insights that could cause harm. That too was God. Second, a new generation came forward that took it upon themselves to confront the powers of darkness, not understanding some truths this book series is expounding on. I believe through closer examination and the combat experience I have had, that God stepped in and shut it down.

Rarely will intercessors see a fallen angel from the second heaven. Intercessors do not go into the second heaven in spiritual warfare, but the Holy Spirit takes them into the spirit realm. The intercessor's conflict with second heaven fallen angels, known as thrones, dominions, principalities, and powers, are more about pushing back the darkness.

The darkness is their influence over the earth and their abilities to blind the minds of mankind. The travailing intercessor partners with the Holy Spirit only and together they push back the influence of the evil ruling territorial spirit. Depending on the intercessor and how much the intercessor can yield to the Holy Spirit through takeover, determines the dimension in which the intercessor will operate. The intercessor must learn what I call, "how to get out of the Holy Spirit's way." The Holy Spirit will take the intercessor over to confront second heaven territorial fallen angels.

There are certain travailing intercessors who are called to team up with the Holy Spirit in the earth over individuals, churches, cities, regions, states, nations, global to push back the power or the influence of fallen angels. Any intercessor that believes they have the authority to engage a fallen angel prophetically in prayer over regions has clearly strayed from the truth. Therefore, we know that that intercessor has never been in a direct hand to hand combat encounter with fallen angels.

When we look at Matthew 6:10, we see that heaven is to come to earth. "Your kingdom come, Your will be done on earth as it is in heaven." We also see in Job 2:2, Satan, who can be a metaphor for the fallen angels, answers God's question: 'The Lord said to Satan, "From where have you come?" Then Satan answered the Lord, "From roaming around on the earth and from walking around on it."' I like the answer Satan gives God according to the NLT, 'Satan answered the Lord, "I have been patrolling the earth, watching everything that's going on.'"

Was not the Holy Spirit sent to the believers in the earth? God the Holy Spirit was sent from heaven to earth. Psalm 115:16 (NLT) says, "The heavens belong to the Lord, but he has given the earth to all humanity." Notice our boundaries! In over one thousand second heaven deliverances, it is the fallen angels who come down, on their own accord or by a direct order from God. What does Revelation 12:7-8 says, "Then there was war in heaven. Michael and his angels fought against the dragon and his angels. And the dragon lost the battle, and he and his angels were forced out of heaven." Any student of the Bible can plainly see that it is the angels who war in the second heaven, not mankind going up into the second heaven with some special authority. It was the Holy Spirit who took the Apostles John and Paul up; they did not go into the second heaven, but the third.

Jesus came to earth, He came down, and His mission was to draw human beings back into fellowship with the Father, and He was willing to die on the cross so it could be possible. His focus was on people, and the devil's kingdom was one obstacle, although a formidable one, standing in the way of human redemption. We should not believe that we should see spiritual warfare as an end in itself. Without prayer, power evangelism, and discipleship, spiritual warfare alone cannot get the job done.

A church or a prayer group who thinks they can take authority against a fallen angel over a city and his lesser demonic spirits have never been in a face-to-face deliverance with a fallen angel. A principality has legal rights to that city because of the sins of man.

> *For you are the children of your father the devil, and you love to do the evil things he does. He was a murderer from the beginning. He has always hated the truth, because there is no truth in him. When he lies, it is consistent with his character; for he is a liar and the father of lies. John 8:44 NLT*

> *But when people keep on sinning, it shows that they belong to the devil, who has been sinning since the beginning. But the Son of God came to destroy the works of the devil. 1 John 3:8 NLT*

We can now conclude that no one man or woman, prayer group or church can take authority over a fallen angel that holds the people through sin captive. I am also talking about the believer as well as the non-believer.

STRATEGIC LEVEL INTERCESSION

I need to talk about strategic-level or second heaven intercession. How does a church in a city break free from the control of the fallen angels? As stated in book one of "Exploring Secrets of the Heavenly Realms," the assembly must come together and pray that God would remove the fallen angel who has the right to church growth. The travailing intercessors and the prophetic prayer warriors must come together through prayer and fasting. We must remind God through "it is written" prayers that we are the body of Christ and are called to win our city for Christ.

When a local church comes together and begins to pray and fast over their city, they continue until the leadership and intercessors sense the spiritual powers over the territory have been ordered by God not to resist the spread of the gospel. The visible manifestation for the church is growth. Power evangelism is a key component in this process. If the church will pray and fast and allow the Holy Spirit to move, the powers of darkness must draw back.

The church must use "it is written" to engage in strategic spiritual warfare prayer. Spirit-directed prayer using the scriptures opens the way for the blessings of God to come upon the region with salvations, healings, deliverances, holiness, compassion and love for all who come in need of Jesus. Praise and worship will soar to new heights, and they will all glorify God.

There are two laws that seem to override sin, rebellion, and evil. These laws are, "it is written," quoting scripture and the second, the laws of prayer. These two laws combined have taken out some of the highest ranking fallen angels over churches and family bloodlines. The laws of prayer and quoting the scriptures are the two highest laws of the universe.

The real conflict for effective church growth and evangelism is a spiritual battle. I commented in the opening of this chapter that the reason people are not turning to the Church, and to God for answers is the lack of spiritual power against the kingdom of darkness. If a church does not humble themselves and pray, we lose the spiritual battle. We know thus far that there are two things each church must do so evangelism and growth can work better. When we come together in serious prayer, and the gifted people who are called, and anointed individuals who are powerful in the ministry of intercession, declare the Word of God, breakthrough happens.

We have a deeper revelation on how Satan does indeed assign a fallen angel and divisions of demons to every territorial region in the world, and that they are among the principalities and powers against whom we wrestle. What this book series brings forward are the facts about territorial spirits in a new light and calls many church leaders across the theological spectrum to the program and structure of how the fallen angels operate.

As the reader can tell, we have found very few individuals who have what we could consider a professional-level grasp of either the theory or practice of dealing with territorial spirits, and none who combined both. This revelation is seriously missing in the Church today! As I read other authors or listened to spiritual warfare teachers' podcasts, I found very little beyond the standard wisdom that has been accumulated on spiritual warfare in general. If we do not understand how territorial spirits operate and their legal rights, how can we pray effectively? This author has trained and equipped a group of intercessors to do spiritual warfare so they can pray in power and in working knowledge.

Is it not our responsibility as believers in Christ, and stewards of the mysteries of God, to seek answers as to just how Satan and the fallen angels go about veiling the gospel? We are not to be ignorant of the devices of the fallen.

The Church must understand that certain fallen angelic thrones have the ability to patrol the earth and to watch over all the laws and sins mankind live under by their influence. They have the authority to set up shop over any region that threatens their domination and rule. Therefore, certain intercessory prayer meetings can become pretty intense. As the intercessors pray and travail the Word of God, what influence, authority, and control the fallen angelic majesty came with is pushed back. The intercessors feel the power of the Holy Spirit as the group travails, pushing through the weight or the heaviness of darkness.

For we do not wrestle against flesh and blood,
but against principalities, against powers,
against the rulers of the darkness of this age,
against spiritual hosts of wickedness in the
heavenly places. Ephesians 6:12 NKJV

We are to expose the works of darkness through power ministry and prayer. Not only do we learn how evil works, but we grow in a deeper understanding of who Jesus is. By defeating the multi-tiered kingdom of darkness the way Jesus did, we learn authority and the power of prayer.

For our wrestling match is not against flesh and blood [contending only with physical opponents], not against persons with bodies, but against cosmic powers or fallen angels within four levels of the celestial realm who rule in various areas and in descending orders of authority. Against world dominators of this present evil age, and against spiritual forces of wickedness in the heavenlies who have tiered authority.

My definition of Ephesians 6:12 shows how Satan delegates high-ranking members of the hierarchy of fallen angels to control nations, regions, cities, tribes, people groups, neighborhoods, and other significant social networks of human beings throughout the world.

This pictures a very highly structured organization of levels and grades according to numbers within a hierarchy who are well organized as a kingdom of four different dimensions in the second heaven. These different kinds of fallen angels within each of the four dimensions have descending orders of authorities and different rulers and sub-rulers according to their grade and number. These fallen angels are responsible for different areas of authority in the second heaven and rule over the earth through the minds of mankind.

Let us work through Paul's account of spiritual warfare. First is the word 'our'! This refers to something that will be done throughout this evil age. It will be the churches and the individual Christian's struggle with the levels of the devil's kingdom. Wrestling is a contest between two in which each endeavors to throw the other, and which is decided when the victor can hold down his opponent with his hand upon his neck.

This definition is a match or a contest between the fallen angels and individuals, intercessors, and churches that compete against each other. Jesus defeated the devil in the wilderness with the words, "it is written." Travailing intercessors must pray the Word of God and have the Holy Spirit manifest His power through them.

These revelations are not only biblical definitions, but definitions explained through power encounters and countless prayer meetings. Fallen angels desire to interlace or weave their thoughts into the minds of humanity to steer and control the movement and course of this evil age. It is the job of the Church to power evangelize and to call believers, intercessors, and leaders to hold all night prayer meetings; to prayer walk their cities.

I have noticed within prayer meetings, the degree of resistance the fallen angels bring upon the group is the level of breakthrough contested for. If local churches prayed over their district like Church In One Accord is doing, the resistance will weaken and the receptivity to the gospel will spread.

FALLEN ANGEL RESISTANCE

The title Satan means the one who resists or opposes. Satan is often used in scripture as a metaphor for the fallen angels. They are the ones who resist and oppose God's purposes and the spread of the gospel. The fallen angels try to prevent through actions, prayer meetings, church attendance, the spread of the gospel, and the supernatural work of the Holy Spirit. The fallen are the adversary or the resisters who oppose churches in every region.

The New Testament title of the devil and the fallen means the slanderer or the accuser. Why is this name so appropriate? Because the main weapon Satan and fallen angels is to use against us is accusation.

The Word of God shows us that at his creation Satan was not Satan as we know him presently. He was Lucifer, one of the chief archangels of God, outstanding both for his beauty and his wisdom. Apparently he was in charge of one third of all the created angels. This is an amazing revelation because it hints at the ranking and creative order in which God made each angel.

When the rebellion occurred, they were ejected from heaven, Lucifer (now Satan, the opposer) set up his own rival kingdom in another area of the universe—what the Bible refers to as the heavenlies or sometimes the mid-heaven. The heavenlies are situated somewhere between earth and the heaven of God's throne—and they are the location of Satan's headquarters in this age. In the heavenlies he rules over the large company of rebellious angels. The four levels with many sub-levels within the four dimensions of his kingdom are thrones, dominions, principalities, and powers.

CHAPTER TWO

Satans supreme purpose is to resist and prevent God's purposes and God's people, primarily through sin, slander and accusation. It is the responsibility of the people of God to promote righteousness, prayerfulness, churches who evangelize, and to use "it is written" in the Word of God.

For we are not fighting against people made of flesh and blood, but against persons without bodies—the evil rulers of the unseen world, those mighty satanic beings and great evil princes of darkness who rule this world; and against huge numbers of wicked spirits in the spirit world. Ephesians 6:12 TLB

The Bible locates the fallen angels in the second heaven and in the spirit world. This defines the nature of our warfare and the conflict in which we are engaged. Unless we understand this, we cannot possibly be fully successful engaging in prayer and power evangelism. When were you at a prayer meeting when the group asked God to send down a fallen angel that is resisting your church for judgment? Most Church leaders would not even know if a fallen angel came down on their own authority to block, withstand, and combat the prayer meeting. I would say from experience and biblical definition, that prayerlessness, division, and slander are signs of a fallen angel influence, if not presence.

When the Most High gave to the nations their inheritance, when he divided mankind, he fixed the borders of the peoples according to the num-

ber of the sons of God. Deuteronomy 32:8 ESV

Understanding that evil is not something but someone is a crucial weapon for warfare prayer in the spiritual realm. Knowing this, we can understand and counter the fallen's most successful tactics against us. Every prayer meeting faces the fallen angel that has been assigned to work against a church. The intercessors face territorial fallen angels who cover districts and oversee each fallen angel assigned to each church. Every prayer meeting knows from scripture that the territorial fallen angel over the city supervises every fallen angel within his sphere of authority; I would call them city limits and districts within.

Each church leader should ask themselves what has God told you about the church's mission and why is it not coming to pass. Could it be because there is a fallen angel assigned to withstand your mission. Mega churches who do not move in the power of God witness with their own eyes the assignment of the fallen angel who is opposing the move of the Holy Spirit through the minds of men. Church growth without power means man's agenda. This was never the design of the early Church.

Every leader, intercessor, and church elder should understand what the word anti-christ means. The definition is one who opposes Christ, implying the usurping of Christ and His position. This has already happened in most churches today. The gospel is preached, but there is no manifestation of the Holy Spirit to enforce the rule of Christ. This is the work of a fallen angel who is assigned to keep the power of God out of the church. Why is that? If there is no travailing intercession, no healing, no deliverance and exorcism, prophesy, and the rest of the gifts of the Spirit, a fallen angel lives over that assembly and is not threatened by removal.

Spiritual warfare has its origin in a rebellion of many angels against God. We see Satan as the prince of this world, leading an array of forces opposed to God. Although disarmed by Jesus Christ on the cross, they remain a powerful threat to the church and to individual believers. Jesus ordered the Church with the great commission. To disarm is to take away the weapons from the fallen angels and render them harmless through judgment. A church can deprive a territorial fallen angel of its work by following the guidelines set up in the book of Acts. Territorial fallen angels continually harassed Paul through the minds of men, yet he preached the gospel, people were saved, and signs and wonders were visible signifying God's approval. This is a great mystery, God's power and Satan's power can cohabitate in the same region, church, and believer.

Chapter Three

A Well Organized Army

The warfare believers must fight is spiritual, personal, intense and continual. It calls for courage, determination and prayer, and therefore believers must stand in God's strength and use the armor he has provided. Spiritual warfare has its origin in a rebellion of many angels against God. Satan is seen as the prince of this world, leading an array of forces opposed to God.

> *For He rescued us from the domain of darkness, and transferred us to the kingdom of His beloved Son, Colossians 1:13 NASB*

The word domain is another word for authority and is understood by the authority necessary to exercise such dominion. For some simple theology, we are now rescued spiritually from the authority of the fallen angels, yet because we still have a sin nature, the Adamic nature, on that day, the day of Christ's return, we will be mentally and physically set free. The word domain or authority comes from the meaning of a region of the earth. Regions of the earth have to do with geographical areas. The territorial fallen angels who are higher in the ranking structure of principalities have jurisdictions according to physical features of an area or geography.

I live in Texas, so let us use the Red River for an example. The Red River runs through the states of Texas and Oklahoma, but also covers parts of New Mexico, Arkansas and Louisiana. Since the Red River separates most of the state of Texas and Oklahoma, that is the jurisdictional rule and authority of a fallen angel. Depending on the structure, this ruling fallen angel is probably a dominion in the four levels of the second heaven and according to the population will determine his number or ranking.

There are a couple of relationships or types of words that domain shares; they are hometown and wilderness. This, too, is territorial jurisdictional boundaries. Each church is responsible for its area or sphere of authority. We are to pray over our area of responsibility, evangelize and serve that area.

CHAPTER THREE

Two Opposing Kingdoms

There are different pictures of God's people in the New Testament. We see some of those pictures in the book of Ephesians as a legislative assembly, a family, a temple, and as the bride of Christ. However, there is one more picture in the book of Ephesians that most believers have not stepped into; it is that of an army.

God has called this army to fight a war that is global or I could even say universal in its proportions. A war that affects and encompasses every portion of the earth in which we live. Not only has every church on this globe been called into this war, meaning every church engaging in spiritual warfare by casting out demons; but each church is to engage in spiritual warfare prayer.

The adjective that correctly describes this battle with the fallen angels and their demonic infantry army is universal. This battle on earth, God has given the church authority and power to cast out demons, but with the fallen angels, God has called us to a wrestling match. Simply put, our wrestling match is with the nature of the fallen angels, sin! The reader may say, that seems to be simple. As I have said before in this book series, fallen angels draw their strength from and control mankind through sin. Demons use sin to gain entry into our lives. This is the basis for spiritual warfare.

For this reason, because I have heard of your faith
in the Lord Jesus and your love for all God's people,

I do not cease to give thanks for you, remembering you in my prayers; [I always pray] that the God of our Lord Jesus Christ, the Father of glory, may grant you a spirit of wisdom and of revelation [that gives you a deep and personal and intimate insight] into the true knowledge of Him [for we know the Father through the Son]. And [I pray] that the eyes of your heart [the very center and core of your being] may be enlightened [flooded with light by the Holy Spirit], so that you will know and cherish the hope [the divine guarantee, the confident expectation] to which He has called you, the riches of His glorious inheritance in the saints (God's people), and [so that you will begin to know] what the immeasurable and unlimited and surpassing greatness of His [active, spiritual] power is in us who believe. These are in accordance with the working of His mighty strength which He produced in Christ when He raised Him from the dead and seated Him at His own right hand in the heavenly places, far above all rule and authority and power and dominion [whether angelic or human], and [far above] every name that is named [above every title that can be conferred], not only in this age and world but also in the one to come. And He put all things [in every realm] in subjection under Christ's feet, and appointed Him as [supreme and authoritative] head over all things in the church, which is His body, the fullness of Him who fills and completes all things in all [believers]. Ephesians 1:15-23

Paul begins this portion of scripture with thanking God for this body of believers. He prays that God, through the Holy Spirit, would give to the Ephesian believers wisdom and revelation that gives them deep and personal and intimate insight into the true knowledge of Him, to know the Father through the Son. In other words, Paul prays that the Ephesians would completely understand this new creation called the new man in Christ Jesus.

Paul was truly a prayer warrior—remembering the churches in his personal prayers: for example, the Romans (Romans 1:9), the Philippians (Philippians 1:3-4), the Colossians (Colossians 1:3-4), and the Thessalonians (1 Thessalonians 1:2-3).

He prayed that our heart or the very center and core of our being (new creation) would come into a revelation of what God has done in Christ Jesus concerning the new creation. Paul is praying that the believer's new personality, it would flood the center of thought and moral judgment with truth so we could see the reality of our future now. The ability to live in Christ Jesus' resurrection power now, not just in the Age to come. Paul says, the Holy Spirit has been given the task of imparting this glorious inheritance to the believer now. The believer would live under the blessings of the Age to come now, demonstrating the power of that Age. The Holy Spirit was urging Paul to pray that the divine guarantee or the full inheritance of the new creation with all its riches indwelled in Christ Jesus would begin to operate in the believer.

Paul now shifts his prayer toward defeating the kingdom of darkness that opposes this glorious new creation through the sinful nature. Paul says, the Holy Spirit desires that we will begin to know the immeasurable, unlimited, and surpassing greatness of God's active supernatural power that the believer has inside them. This unlimited power is God's strength which He produced in Christ when He raised Him from the dead. In other words, it is the power of Christ Jesus that overcame this evil age and the gods or the fallen angels of this evil age.

The prayer now changes from the earthly realm to the heavenly realm. That God seated Christ Jesus at His own right hand in the heavenly places, far above all rule and authority and power and dominion [whether angelic or human], and [far above] every name that is named [above every title that can be conferred], not only in this age and world but also in the one to come. Did the reader catch that, "not only in this age but in the Age to come"? Now notice how specifically the Holy Spirit has Paul write. God has put all things [in every realm] in subjection under Christ's feet. In the new creation, God has placed us in Christ Jesus and desires His children to operate as Christ Jesus now operates, in this age and in the Age to come.

The last verse states that we are His body and that we have the ability in us to express the fullness of who Christ Jesus is and through that fullness bring heaven to earth. I could say, through Christ's authority, having all the necessary and appropriate blessings to bring order to the universe, and finish the course or administration that God has ordained in Christ; to complete or finish the total defeat of the kingdom of darkness.

We assist this revelation and growth of the new creation as the believer engages in the supernatural, doing what Jesus commanded us to do. We are to heal the sick, raise the dead, cleanse the lepers, cast out demons. By ministering in the supernatural, we are to come into the maturity of the new creation.

This is the power of it is written! Understanding who we are in Christ Jesus and comprehending the words Jesus speaks in Matthew 4:4, "It is written and forever remains written, 'Man shall not live by bread alone, but by every word that comes out of the mouth of God'"(AMP). This is the revelation that defeats the fallen angels. It is God's written word that will forever remain written. When God gives me a scripture to decree and declare it brings judgment down on the fallen angel I'm engaged with. It reveals his guilt before God the Father.

> (as it is written [in Scripture], "I have made you
> a father of many nations") in the sight of Him in
> whom he believed, that is, God who gives life to
> the dead and calls into being that which does not
> exist. In hope against hope Abraham believed that
> he would become a father of many nations, as he
> had been promised [by God]: "So [numberless]
> shall your descendants be." Without becoming
> weak in faith he considered his own body, now as
> good as dead [for producing children] since he was

about a hundred years old, and [he considered] the deadness of Sarah's womb. But he did not doubt or waver in unbelief concerning the promise of God, but he grew strong and empowered by faith, giving glory to God, being fully convinced that God had the power to do what He had promised. Therefore his faith was credited to him as righteousness (right standing with God). Now not for his sake alone was it written that it was credited to him, but for our sake also—to whom righteousness will be credited, as those who believe in Him who raised Jesus our Lord from the dead. Romans 4:17-24 AMP

Paul says, God is the Creator and the giver and supporter of life. He brings the dead back to life and brings into existence what didn't exist before. The God of the impossible is directly tied to as it is written in scripture. Like Abraham, we are to believe God's promises, speak God's promise, and pray God's promises. We are to believe against all hope or beyond all natural hope. When things seem impossible like Abraham's situation, too old to father children, his faith said that God has the ability to fulfill His promises.

Paul assumed every believer knew that they were involved in a war and new they need the armor of God to stand against the fallen angels' schemes. He also concluded that our adversary is the devil and his kingdom, and that all believers would engage in spiritual warfare and prayer. However, in verse twelve we see the nature of the war:

For our wrestling match is not against flesh and blood,

not against persons with bodies, but against rulers with various areas and descending orders of authority, against the world dominators of this present darkness, against spiritual forces of wickedness in the heavenlies. - Derek Prince Translation

My expanded version of Ephesians 6:12 says this: For our wrestling match is not against flesh and blood [contending only with physical opponents], not against persons with bodies, but against cosmic powers or fallen angels within four levels of the celestial realm who rule in various areas and in descending orders of authority. Against world dominators of this present evil age, and against spiritual forces of wickedness in the heavenlies who have tiered authority.

This pictures a very highly structured organization of levels and grades according to numbers within a hierarchy who are well organized as a kingdom of four different dimensions in the second heaven. These different fallen angels within each of the four dimensions have descending orders of authorities and different rulers and sub-rulers according to their grade and number. These fallen angels are responsible for different areas of authority in the second heaven and rule over the earth through the minds of mankind.

What I have uncovered so far is that there are four second heaven dimensions called angelic majesties and I will give them in order of importance. First, there are thrones, then dominions, next principalities and last, powers. Within each of these levels, at least nine different classes of angels operate. They are ranked and tiered according to their creation date and grade level. This ranking, grade or category, and creation date determines if they operate as a world dominator or to dominate a single bloodline. I use the word dominator because it describes the power and command influence the fallen angels exercise and control through sin.

In Deuteronomy 4:19 Moses says there are the hosts of heaven or the heavenly bodies filled with the vast multitude of different angels set up as a military army with campaign-like operations intended to achieve certain objectives. They seek the goal of these objectives through a multi-level army campaign that is offensive in nature through different maneuvers and strategies, individually, organizationally, territorially and globally.

The sense of the definition comes from an army's practice of taking the field for battle. It also conveys the thought of conquering for the purpose of setting up a fortress within these different areas. The Ephesians 6 account says darkness is of this age (fallen age) and also says "hosts" of wickedness are located in the heavenly places. Hosts is an Old Testament term for fallen angels - Acts 7:42 - O.T. also calls angels the army of heaven or stars of heaven, even terms that symbolize various supernatural powers in the heavenly realms.

Let us read the Living Bible's version of Ephesian 6:12 which is more of a paraphrase:

> *For we are not fighting against people made*
> *of flesh and blood, but against persons without*
> *bodies—the evil rulers of the unseen world, those*
> *mighty satanic beings and great evil princes of*
> *darkness who rule this world; and against huge*
> *numbers of wicked spirits in the spirit world.*

We can clearly see as Christians we are in a battle of enormous proportions and if not taken in proper order could become overwhelming. The order that I am proposing is to call our individual church to prayer. The majority of the church must surrender their lifestyle and come and pray. Once most of the church attends three prayer meetings a week, then it is time to evangelize. What we are seeking is to change our spiritual climate within the church so it overflows into the city.

Climate plays a huge part in where we decide to live, how we dress, what we eat, and which recreational activities we take part in. Just consider what a powerful effect a spiritual climate would have on a city. A godly climate allows people to live peaceful and quiet lives in all godliness and holiness. In first Timothy 2:1-9, Pauls first directive is to petition, then prayers, intercession and thanksgiving be made for all people. To petition is more than an urgent request to God; it is a formal written request and is signed by many people. In other words, the church goes together and agrees in prayer concerning the written Word of God. The church must come to God with a formal request according to "it is written."

Next, Paul instructs us to pray. Prayer is more than a reverent petition or more than speaking to God; first it is a request for help and second it is an expression of thanks. We come to God and ask for His help, acknowledging that we are helpless against the fallen angels of this evil Age. We are to thank God for hearing our prayers because we are praying according to "it is written."

Paul the calls the church to intercede. Intercession defined from the Holman Illustrated Bible Dictionary is an act of intervening or mediating between differing parties, particularly the act of praying to God on behalf of another person. In the OT the Hebrew verb pagaʿ is used of such pleading or interceding (Gen. 23:8; Isa. 53:12; 59:16; Jer. 7:16; 15:11; 27:18; 36:25). More general terms such as palal, "pray," or chalah, "appease," are also sometimes translated "intercede" (1 Sam. 7:5; 1 Kings 13:6). In the NT the Greek term is entungkano and its derivatives (Rom. 8:26–27, 34; 1 Tim. 2:1; Heb. 7:25). I will let my wife give the reader more than a definition, but years of experience in travailing intercession.

Then Paul tells us what to pray for in the remaining verses. If we are to see our city increase in godliness, ungodliness and laws that promote sin must decrease. If this does not happen, we will not see radical transformations in the spiritual climate of our city. We must remember, the fallen angels have established strongholds in our city through years of sin.

Strongholds are how fallen angels stay in control of a

city. Curses and demon possession or demonization are their two most effective weapons. With curses and sin that brings demonic possession, the fallen angel legal rights and curse is how the church prays. We prayer drive and walk the borders of our city limits, and the district in which our church is located. We are repenting for the institutions or organizations of sin.

When fallen angels move in and take possession of cities, it is because of the people who have surrendered to sin and now those territorial spirits consider those cities their property and guard it as a military fortification or stronghold.

There are three sides to a stronghold described by Paul in 2 Corinthians 10:3-6. The first side or foundation of a stronghold is knowledge. So the first step of a fallen angel stronghold is false knowledge or belief in a lie. I now throw us back to the first chapter of this book and how the devil was trying to deceive Jesus. The second step is imaginations, arguments, or reasoning that agree with the kingdom of darkness. The third and final side is thoughts and the content of what the person is thinking about.

We now understand that a stronghold has its roots in the old self or the old man. The old self is the product of deception, of Satan's lie. That which denies the truth of God's Word. Deception gives birth to lust, perverted damaging desires. When one yields to lust, it produces sin, and sin, when it takes its course, produces death. This is the scriptural degenerative process of the old man. The old man has two distinctive characteristics: first, it is corrupt (spiritually, morally, and physically); Second, it is a rebel. This is the birthing ground for fallen angelic strongholds. The fallen deceive as many individuals as possible so they can influence sinful organizations and laws to fortify and strengthen their grip on a city.

Let us look at Romans 6:6-8 on how Jesus has set us free.

"We know that our old sinful selves were crucified with Christ so that sin might lose its power in our lives. We are no longer slaves to sin. For when we died with Christ we were set free from the power of sin. And since we died with Christ, we know we will also live with him."

I have found that most Christians don't know the truth about the old self and the new self. This is where the kingdom of darkness on all levels takes advantage of believers. First, Paul reveals positional Christianity by stating that those who are born again were crucified with Christ. This is also called substitutional Christianity. Simply put, Jesus died in my place, so I'm to believe and no longer live for myself. If each church understood the true reality of this scripture and the book series, the atmosphere or spiritual climate would be completely different. God would move in more power and many would come to Christ.

When Paul states that the body of sin, the old self, might be done away with, that is conditional. What Paul is driving at is that the fallen angels would no longer have legal rights through the sinful nature. Mankind would pass laws that would expel the fallen. Notice Paul uses the word might, and it is a word that expresses possibility! This means that there is a sanctification process that must transpire. Paul says that as we go through sanctification, sin loses its power.

Positionally, we have the new self, which is free from sin's power and not enslaved to sin and the fallen angels. Verse 7 states that he who has died—died to what?—the old self, and the fallen angel's influence. We believe that we shall (present/future) live with Him. So, the only way of escape from the slavery of sin and the authority of the fallen angels is to crucify the old lower nature called the old man. Because of Jesus, we don't have to be under the influence of the lower nature, which in the doorway to the fallen angels.

Therefore, God has called this army to fight a war that is global or I could even say universal in its proportions. A war that affects and encompasses every portion of the earth in which we live. We know fallen angels draw their strength and control mankind through sin. We know that prayer shifts climates toward defeating the kingdom of darkness that opposes this glorious new creation through the sinful nature. Believers can now use the words it is written and forever remains written in spiritual warfare prayer. When "it is written" is declared, prayed, and acted on, the first step of a fallen angel stronghold collapses because false knowledge or belief in a lie is being opposed. When prayer and evangelism tear down false imaginations, arguments, or reasoning that agree with the kingdom of darkness, the stronghold gives way further. The complete destruction of the stronghold comes when churches, prayer meetings, and evangelism transform the false thoughts and the content of what each person is thinking about transforms the mind of that city.

CHAPTER FOUR

THE POWER OF DECLARATION

When we declare the Word of God at the start of a meeting, a prayer group or praying for people, it makes a tremendous difference in the spiritual atmosphere and the anointing. Let me give a quick definition of the word "declare." The meaning is "to make known," "set forth," rather than (the older meaning) "to explain." It also has a powerful meaning in giving a full account to. We could even interchange the word declare for the verb proclamation. It comes from the Latin word, which means to shout forth. The two most common words the New Testament relates are to confess and to proclaim.

Let us first look at the word confession. The word confession means to say the same as. What the Bible teaches is that we are to say the same with our months as God has already said in His Word. We are to make the words of our mouth agree with the Word of God. This is of vital importance when dealing with fallen angels. It is then not I who is speaking, but the Word of God. Therefore, since the Word of God judged the fallen angels, why wouldn't we speak the Word? When we are speaking the Word of God, the authority and power of God is in what we are confessing.

> *So shall My word be that goes forth from My*
> *mouth;*
> *It shall not return to Me void,*
> *But it shall accomplish what I please,*
> *And it shall prosper in the thing for*
> *which I sent it. - Isaiah 55:11 NKJV*

In chapter one, we looked at Hebrews 3:1 that said Jesus is our high priest of our confession. I want to revisit this scripture and to bring to light something of vital importance. If we have no confession, we have no high priest. Jesus is our high priest regarding what we confess. Here is what the writer of Hebrews is teaching us. Whatever we believe in our hearts and say with our mouths, whatever the Bible says about us, then we have Jesus as our high priest. If we have no confession, then we have no high priest. Remember, we are talking about "it is written."

> *Knowing this first, that no prophecy of Scrip-*
> *ture is of any private interpretation, for*
> *prophecy never came by the will of man, but*

> *holy men of God spoke as they were moved by*
> *the Holy Spirit. 2 Peter 1:20-21 NKJV*

The Bible is the spoken Word of God written as the Holy Spirit moved the writers. If we remain silent, not confessing the Word of God written by the Holy Spirit through man, we shut off the ministry of Jesus as high priest. When we choose to make wrong confessions, we can release the kingdom of darkness to attack whatever we confess. As I have said before, when I quote the Word of God to a fallen angel that is being judged concerning a matter, instantly they are guilty before God and His court. It was the fallen angels who first transgressed God's laws. Therefore, the Old Testament law is so important today for the believer. We are not judged by the law spiritually, but the law reveals mankind's sin through the carnal nature.

> *But the Law came to increase and expand*
> *[the awareness of] the trespass [by defining*
> *and unmasking sin]. But where sin increased,*
> *[God's remarkable, gracious gift of] grace [His*
> *unmerited favor] has surpassed it and in-*
> *creased all the more, Romans 5:20 AMP*

Let us not get stuck in legalism or some idea of incorrect theology. When we accepted Jesus as our savior, our spirit became born again, and God gave us a new nature. Yet our bodies still carry the curse of sin and responses to sin. It is the mind that must go through the transformation process. For a believer to think any differently is to have incorrect theology. I do from time to time make absolutes and some may not like it.

The Bible defines a spoken declaration as aggressive; It is a word of spiritual warfare. When we declare, it is releasing the authority and power of God's Word into the earth. This affects our life, the life of the Church, and the universe. The greatest and most effective way to release the power of God into a situation is to declare God's Word. In our intercessory prayer meetings, when we have a prophetic declaration, it sets off the travailing intercessors. The intercessors will feel the power of what they declare in scripture and the Holy Spirit will pray through them. It is the job of the intercessor to become one with the Holy Spirit through the power of agreement. We have learned that the intercessors are to pray through or continue in travail until joy comes; we call that breakthrough. This happens time after time in our intercessory prayer meetings.

To declare is the activity of a herald, and it is a word we use little today. A herald was someone who had authority from a King, Duke, Nobleman or someone in government. There is one reference in our Bible that makes this meaning very clear.

> *Now as they heard these things, He spoke an-*
> *other parable, because He was near Jerusa-*
> *lem and because they thought the kingdom*
> *of God would appear immediately. There-*
> *fore He said: "A certain nobleman went into*
> *a far country to receive for himself a king-*
> *dom and to return. Luke 19:11-12 NKJV*

When declaring the Word of God for rulership, notice how the people listened to the proclaimed teachings of Jesus which brought about Zaccheus' salvation. The nobleman did not go away to get a realm, an area over which to rule, but a kingdom. Therefore, the realm before Him was the realm in which He intends to rule? The territory in which He was decreeing the Word of God, that territory He would rule over. In the parable, he was no king and so he had no authority. He needed authority, which is the right to rule and the power to exercise that right. So Jesus went off to be crowned King over all, and His kingship would have authority over all. When we look at the Revised Standard Version, it translates the word authority as "kingly power."

It is our job as heralds to go out into our cities with a declaration concerning the will and decisions of God. We are to decree to the rulers and authorities over our cities the will and decisions of God. We are to announce God's will and to pray His decisions into existence. We are to call those things that are not as though they are in prayer. In ancient times, the proclaimer would stand up and say o'yeah, o'yeah, and then make the declaration. In those days, everybody when hearing o'yeah, o'yeah, would stand to attention and listen to the voice of authority speaking to us. When I decree the Word of God to the fallen angels in a deliverance session, they are forced to hear it and obey it.

We now know the Kingdom of God is His kingship, His rule, His authority. When we come to this realization, the Church will execute God's will and decisions territorially, weakening the fallen angels by casting out demons; their foot soldiers. We will go through the New Testament and find passages of scripture evident in establishing God's reign in our cities.

When we come across the word "preach" in the Bible, it is the word of a herald. The meaning is to proclaim, and it is an official or public announcement of what God considers important. The herald is declaring a state of being and reality to assert the manifested authority and power of the king. It is the written law of God.

"And this gospel of the kingdom will be preached throughout the whole world, as a testimony to all nations; and then the end will come" (Matt. 24:14 RSV). We could say, according to definition, that this gospel of the kingdom will be proclaimed or declared. The Bible sense of the Lexicon means to be heralded or to become known publicly and loudly as important news announced by a herald. The reason I have been writing on the second heaven and fallen angels is that I am a proclaimer, a Bible teacher, and my duty is to interpret the Bible and explain supernatural encounters so people can understand. It is time as a Bible expositor, to unravel the mysteries of the second heaven and fallen angels that seem to be unknown, complicated, or theories to almost everyone. Therefore, I entitled my first book, "Exploring Secrets of the Heavenly Realms: Mysteries of the Second Heaven Explained."

My job as a preacher is to translate in a scholarly form the supernatural activities encountered through the deliverance and healing ministry. It is like an artist who is painting a picture, sketching in different parts of the drawing as the mosaic takes place. I am taking patterns found in twenty-two years of supernatural ministry and producing through biblical study secrets of the kingdom of darkness that have not totally been understood. I feel like the author Luke, who gave a report of all that Jesus did and taught. "The first account I made, Theophilus, was [a continuous report] about all the things that Jesus began to do and to teach." My mission that God has given to me is to be a correspondent on all that God has revealed through me in biblical study and supernatural encounters.

I have learned, the Word of God proclaimed in faith, brings enormous power. The secret to seeing the power of God is to preach an excellent gospel and in so doing, having marvelous results. God said to Moses in Exodus 4:11, "So the Lord said to him, "Who has made man's mouth?" Notice how practical God is with Moses. What do you have in your hand? "Now put your hand in your bosom." Then God declares to Moses, "if they do not believe even these two signs, or listen to your voice, that you shall take water from the river and pour it on the dry land. The water which you take from the river will become blood on the dry land." Everything God asked of Moses did not seem particularly important. This is the proclamation of the Word, in prayer, on the streets of the city. All God wants is a vessel! Moses learned that in the things that God asks us to do, there is a potential that far exceeds our own understanding and even beyond our earthly ability. We can do the whole job with the Word of God. When we examine the whole chapter and the book of Exodus, the entire deliverance of Israel was achieved through Moses' rod. We have in our Bible the rod of God, and we can rest in believing God will intervene.

> *Then Jesus answered and said to them, "Most assuredly, I say to you, the Son can do nothing of Himself, but what He sees the Father do; for whatever He does, the Son also does in like manner. For the Father loves the Son, and shows Him all things that He Himself does; and He will show Him greater works than these, that you may marvel. John 5:19-20 NKJV*

Jesus stops what He is saying to comment on what He will say: He could have said, I want you to know. Jesus proclaimed that He could do nothing by Himself, but only what He sees the Father doing. Then Jesus adds a powerful point. He will do it in the way the Father is doing it. Jesus reveals, the only instrument He needed to fulfill His mission was doing what the Father said to do. We are to declare the Word of God in faith, doing as the Father shows us, then the power of God will take over. I see this in healing and deliverance, speaking words of knowledge and seeing the power of God move. Isaiah says it this way, "So will My word be which goes out of My mouth; It will not return to Me void (useless, without result), without accomplishing what I desire, and without succeeding in the matter for which I sent it." (AMP)

The Father loves us, and He desires to show us all the

things He wants us to do. God told Moses, every time you need me to step in and take over use the rod. Jesus says to the New Testament believer, "it is written" so speak the Word of God. The reader should go get their Bible right now and hold it up to God in a prophetic act. Then the believer should declare, my Bible is my rod and I can do everything it says I can do. Do you know that the Bible is a supernatural book, it is the power of God and it is limitless.

SCRIPTURES POWER

The Psalmist says, by the word of the Lord were the heavens made, and all their host by the breath of His mouth (33:6). We see the word heavens, plural, and we define it as the abode of God and the angels. The root definition speaks of supernatural regions and places of supernatural entities. The Bible Lexicon speaks of domains or jurisdictions that include extensions into the natural world. The heavens or heavenly places are regions in the supernatural world with God's angels and fallen angels that extend or have influence over this world.

The Bible gives us a glimpse of the multi-leveled or tiered structure and activity that goes on through spiritual warfare and prayer. Through the scriptures and warfare encounters, I understand that there are many levels (nine as of today) within the four dimensions of the second heaven. There are many classes of angels, both fallen and God's holy angels who are orderly tiered within each dimension of the heavens or heavenly places. Also, God's angels seem to operate in all the heavenly places. I have also found

THE POWER OF DECLARATION

that prayer invokes combat in the second heaven between God's holy angels and the fallen angels. It is the failure of the Church to pray without ceasing that has kept the fallen angels enthroned. This is one of the greatest revelations that I have found in second heaven combat. The Church's job is to force these cosmic fallen angels to come down to defend their various levels and jurisdictions of rule in the earth. What causes the fallen to come down? Asking in prayer! However, it is combat that free's mankind through prayer, power evangelism, and deliverance.

Paul calls himself an apostle, a word whose root means is "to send." This Greek word was first used of a cargo ship or fleet, but later denoted a commander of a fleet. The New Testament uses the word to signify an approved spokesman sent as a personal representative. Although not every Christian is called by God to minister like Paul or the twelve apostles, God sends every Christian to represent Him before the people with whom he or she comes in contact. A commander is a person in authority over a body of troops and the one in charge of military operations. The definition also uses the word as a member of a higher class in some orders of knighthood. My point is, an apostle is a general who leads the Church into combat.

> *"Fight the good fight of the faith [in the conflict with evil]; take hold of the eternal life to which you were called, and [for which] you made the good confession [of faith] in the presence of many witnesses." 1 Timothy 6:12 AMP*

Paul uses the word fight twice. The Greek meaning of the first use of the word is to be engaged in a battle. The definition states that the battle is an ongoing battle. This ongoing battle will be an intense struggle with spiritual forces or fallen angels who through the minds of mankind will establish strong opposition to the things of God. This scripture by definition ties itself to Ephesians 6:12. According to the definition, the first fight is to be engaged in an intense struggle with spiritual forces or fallen angels. The fight or struggle or wrestling match is for leadership over a region. Paul is telling Timothy, the apostolic ministry is in a power struggle for direction or spiritual guidance for the right to control and establish a government in a region. The fallen angels through their military structure in a region, will bring strong opposition through the minds of mankind to contest the apostolic ministry that brings God's government.

Paul notifies Timothy, as we proclaim the gospel, we will enter an intense struggle for the will of man. The gospel will challenge the minds of man and their belief system. This gospel will seek to engage every stronghold and contest every spiritual power, even in the heavenly realms. Paul says, the one who declares the Word of God enters a contest or a competition for the souls in that region. The fallen angelic territorial spirits will oppose the message of the gospel and fight intensely for the souls of man. This fight gets started when most believers in the Church come together in their local assembly and prays. Let me give you an example!

For I want you to know how great a struggle I have for you and for those [believers] at Laodicea, and for all who [like yourselves] have never seen me face to face. Colossians 2:1 AMP

Paul was combating false teaching in the Colossian church similar to Gnosticism (from gnosis, the Greek word for knowledge). Though Gnosticism did not become popular until the second century, even in Paul's day these ideas sounded attractive to many, and exposure to such teachings could easily seduce a church that didn't know Christian doctrine well. Paul struggled, knowing that the false teaching threatened the Colossian Church and believers from maturing in their faith. Paul's contest was against spiritual foes or fallen angels and human adversaries, which were under the fallen's influence and mindset.

The writer of Hebrews uses spiritual warfare terms in Hebrews 12:1, "Therefore, since we have so great a cloud of witnesses surrounding us, let us also lay aside every encumbrance and the sin which so easily entangles us, and let us run with endurance the race that is set before us," (NASB). There are two warfare terms used "encumbrance" and "entangles." However, the Bible Lexicon defines encumbrance as something immaterial that interferes with or delays action or progress; understood as a large and weighty mass. Therefore, it is a hinderance or difficulty of large size. What the writer of Hebrews is telling us is that fallen angels seek to slow down or completely hinder prayer and the spread of the gospel. They also create difficulty, so it restrains the transformation process of the new man. The scripture defines immaterial as disembodied, spiritual, or supernatural. When we put immaterial and interferes together, we have a large quantity of intangible forces that stand in the way or obstruct the progress of the individuals, churches, and the move of the Holy Spirit.

The second spiritual warfare term used is entangles, and it means skillfully encircling all sides to attack, assail, or inhibit action; idea of being in control. Through the vehicle of sin, the fallen angels attack mankind. They seek to engage mankind in a battle; that fight is for righteousness or wickedness. This is the fight, a contest with evil supernatural beings called fallen angels and demonic spirits who take on mankind in a war over morality. Scripture speaks of a wrestling or a contest between the children of light and the evil fallen angels who assign demons to the children of disobedience. Therefore, the contest between the Church and the fallen angels will carry on throughout this evil Age. It is a struggle for power and leadership of individuals, churches, businesses, institutions, cities, counties, states, nations, and the right to lead the universe.

Let us take a city for example. The fallen angels encircle each city as sin spreads. As mankind sins, the volume of fallen angels over the city and the demonic spirits within mankind increases. The Bible calls this a sphere of jurisdiction. Scripture refers to it as spheres of authority or spheres influenced by darkness; They are evil realms controlled by evil fallen angels and give right for demon possession. Jesus tells us in the parable of the wheat and the tares, "Let both grow together until the harvest." This truth is deeper than just the children of light and of darkness. Two kingdoms coexist, the work of light and darkness, righteousness and wickedness, the old man and the new man coexist, all these things that battle for the souls of man coexist.

Paul instructs the body of Christ that this conflict will continue to the end of the Age and each kingdom, whether light or darkness, will seek to hold his opponent down with his hand or power. That hand of power will be placed upon the neck or the right to control his enemy; signaling the defeat of a generation with even more influence over generations to come. This is what the word "wrestling" in Ephesians 6:12 means. Let me end the chapter with expounding deeper into the word "wrestling."

Wrestling is defined as a contest between two in which each endeavors to throw the other, and which is decided when the victor is able to hold his opponent down with his hand upon his neck; and the term is transferred to the Christian's struggle with the power of evil. Paul is telling the body of Christ, if the Church does not learn how to wrestle with the fallen angels, we will be thrown down by evil's power and evil will lead a territory. This is progressive in nature. First we are engaged. We are seeking the presence and power of God, yet we are not seeing the book of Acts in the Church today. We have been engaged by fallen angels. Second, to be throw down is another word for stumble. To stumble is defined as to suffer ruin and to fail or be unsuccessful.

The yoke of my transgressions was bound; They

were woven together by His hands, And thrust upon my neck. He made my strength fail; The Lord delivered me into the hands of those whom I am not able to withstand. Lamentations 1:14 NKJV

The power of sin is too much for mankind to resist. Jeremiah says, because of the transgressions of mankind God has delivered mankind into the hands or power of the fallen angels. Paul is saying, without the knowledge and training to wrestle with fallen angels, the fallen have the ability to unseat God and Christ Jesus as ruler in this evil Age. It is the progressive decent of mankind into sin. Since the turn of the 20th century, we have seen evil spread throughout the earth, generation after generation. We have seen an increase in the depths of sin. We also have had an increase in ungodly laws that establish sin in society. If the believers do not learn to wrestle with fallen angels, the Holy Spirit through the Church will not restrain the coming of the anti-christ. When the war starts in the second heaven between Michael and his angels verses the devil and his angels, when they are cast to the earth, will you be able to defeat them or will you be persecuted and then martyred?

CHAPTER FIVE

IT IS WRITTEN - BRUCE

I n this book series, we have learned that Satan delegates high-ranking members of the hierarchy of fall-
en angels to control nations, regions, cities, tribes,
people groups, neighborhoods, and other significant social networks of human beings worldwide. Therefore, we will examine Colossians 2:8 and 2:20, and the
Greek word "stoicheion" which means elemental spirits or
power; heavenly supernatural powers over the world; the
supernatural powers or forces regarded as having control
over the events of this world. This also reflects the Greek
term "cosmos," which points to spiritual beings.

*See to it that no one takes you captive through phi-
losophy and empty deception [pseudo-intellectual
babble], according to the tradition [and musings]*

of mere men, following the elementary principles
of this world, rather than following [the truth—
the teachings of] Christ. Colossians 2:8 AMP

Paul is warning the church at Colossae about deceptive philosophy or intellectualism. There is a lot of that coming out of seminaries today. Graduates who are told what the Bible says instead of experiencing the power of God's Word. I love theology and scriptural study, but as you read my book series, the reader must conclude that the supernatural power of God is a part of study. In his warning, Paul encourages the believer to stay away from the exercise of the intellect or the theory that knowledge is wholly or mainly derived from pure reason. Paul calls this practice empty and deceiving. Even in most supernatural schools of ministry, by their reasoning, they have produced captives. These schools embrace the healing side of God, but not the delivering power of exorcism. Whichever highway a person may have traveled, these schools are creating believers whose minds have been confined or controlled by the school's belief system.

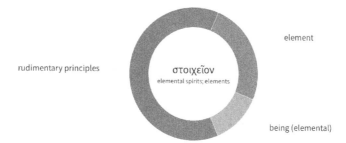

What Paul is saying is the same thing the writer of Hebrews is saying in 5:12, "For though by this time you ought to be teachers [because of the time you have had to learn these truths], you actually need someone to teach you again the elementary principles of God's word [from the beginning], and you have come to be continually in need of milk, not solid food"(AMP). I always like to dig deeper into definition, it has produced my theology on fallen angels as I have encountered them through combat experience. The surface meaning here reveals something was blocking their ability to learn and grow in the simple doctrines of the Christian faith. The Lexham Theological Wordbook says, στοιχεῖον (stoicheion). n. neut. is an elemental power or elemental spirit. A kind of supernatural force. Now let me give the reader one more scripture before I make my point:

> *But even if our gospel is veiled, it is veiled to those who are perishing, 4 whose minds the god of this age has blinded, who do not believe, lest the light of the gospel of the glory of Christ, who is the image of God, should shine on them. 2 Corinthians 4:3-4 NKJV*

In four of the seven instances, the scripture uses the term to show the "elemental forces" in the world against which the believer must struggle (Gal 4:3, 9; Col 2:8, 20). Although the term is impersonal, it conveys a sense of supernatural power and a will to direct earthly events. We learned from chapter four that a struggle is a contest with evil spirit beings to unseat God or the knowledge of God.

Therefore, fallen angels resist believers in learning God's Word. They blind believers' minds so they cannot see the glory of God in the face of Christ Jesus. The writer of Hebrews rebukes these believers for not dealing with the fallen angels and territorial spirits. The fallen angels oversee and order the restriction of God's Word, but it is the demons who are assigned to carry out the assignment. We also know from the theological wordbook that there are supernatural powers desiring to direct earthly events and the course of this Age.

The Bible defines darkness as the sphere dominated by evil, sinfulness, and ignorance of God and His ways. The scripture also describes it as the absence of light. Accordingly, the ruling fallen angel over each territory works relentlessly to keep a tight control on the spread of the gospel, any prayer movement, and uses any doorway to the mind that resists the outpouring of the Holy Spirit. The fallen angels within a specific sphere or territory keep a controlling influence over man through the sin which controls us so tightly. The reader might ask, what is the answer?

A warrior filled with wisdom ascends into the high place and releases regional breakthrough, bringing down the strongholds the mighty. 23 Watch your words and be careful what you say, and you'll be surprised how few troubles you'll have. Proverbs 21:22-23 Passion Translation

There are so many believers who think they are spiritual warriors. They say, "I'm a deliverance minister or I'm a prayer warrior." So let us see if this is true. The Bible Lexicon defines a warrior as someone engaged in or experienced in warfare. The definition goes deeper, and it is one who is military minded. A trained soldier who engages in war. To be honest, I don't know very many prayer warriors who engage the forces of darkness in prayer manifesting unto deliverance. I haven't run across very many prayer meetings that bring about combat. Let me say it this way, a prayer meeting that brings the forces of darkness out into the open the be dealt with. The Bible Lexicon defines a warrior as someone who is trusted. That means warfare will follow you! God will continue to bring people to you who need prayer that brings deliverance and exorcism. I also don't know very many deliverance ministers who have left the classroom and stepped out on the battlefield to confront the Goliaths, which is a type and shadow of the fallen angels.

There is another definition for a warrior and that is a champion. A champion is a believer who is militarily minded and who is trained in the art of war so that those who have placed him in authority can trust him. He is a warrior and exceptional in combat. He is one who has been entrusted to lead troops into war and to represent the army in dueling combat. The definition calls a champion a commander. We know from the last chapter that a commander is a general. He holds a position of authority and command. This is what the fallen angels see when God has raised up a champion, a believer who can represent the body of Christ in dueling combat against the fallen angels.

To be fully trained means to operate out of the wisdom God has revealed to you. This is what this book series is all about, the wisdom of God.

> *So now through the church the multifaceted*
> *wisdom of God [in all its countless aspects]*
> *might now be made known [revealing the mys-*
> *tery] to the [angelic] rulers and authorities in*
> *the heavenly places. Ephesians 3:10 AMP*

With every power encounter and every definition study through scripture, God's power and His Word is saying, "it is written," God is showing us His wisdom and intelligence with every supernatural encounter. He is revealing scripture and power encounters to increase man's discernment and intelligence. God is desiring the Church to take on these supernatural powers in the heavenly places. He wants us to know that the fallen angels are fighting for control of this world and an ongoing battle for events now.

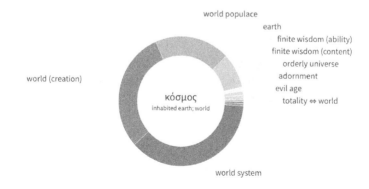

God has released to the Church His next move, and that is to deal with the fallen angelic majesties. Fallen Angels have their own world system of values, beliefs, and morals that are in direct rebellion to God. This affects the individual, people groups, states, and nations.

> *"If you have died with Christ to the elementary principles of the world, why, as if you were still living in the world, do you submit to rules and regulations." Colossians 2:20 AMP*

Paul is telling the Colossians, since you have died with Christ, why are you letting the supernatural powers or forces of fallen angels have control over the events of this church and city. Why are people turning to festivals, new moon or a Sabbath day, false humility, and the worship of fallen angels? He says, anything outside of Christ Jesus will jeopardize your freedom. God is restoring to the Church this struggle for the leadership of churches and cities. We must look at this battle as an ongoing competition to attain positional control for the right to rule. If there is no move of the Holy Spirit as in the book of Acts, that city must struggle for an outpouring.

Moving back to where this all started, a warrior filled with wisdom ascends into the high place. The warrior does not leave his battlefield, but God sends the fallen down to be judged because that champion has led his people into a place that demands judgment. What is a regional breakthrough? When realms and territories of darkness that have been dominated by evil and sinfulness turns to Jesus.

This is when the Holy Spirit wipes away the ignorance of God and His ways, and floods that region with light and power. Where there was the absence of light, now there is nothing but light. We push the fallen angels spheres of authority back by the spread of the gospel in power. The influence of darkness that had realms of control over a city is broken by the bringing down of every stronghold in the city.

We are to watch our words carefully, remembering how Jesus defeated the devil in the wilderness and how Michael the archangel spoke to the devil. In each case, the Word of God or the Father Himself spoke. Jesus quoted the written Word. Michael asks God for a rebuke. The promise is that if we speak properly, we will have very little trouble with the fallen angels when God sends them down for judgment. Not every fallen angel encounter will be the same. The definition states that there are spheres of authority and spheres of darkness. These are realms in the second heaven that have different levels of fallen angels.

Remember what I wrote in my other three books on "Exploring Secrets of the Heavenly Realms," that this pictures a very highly structured organization of levels and grades according to numbers within a hierarchical organization that is systematic (structured) as a kingdom of four different dimensions in the second heaven. These different fallen angels are within each of the four dimensions have descending orders of authorities and different rulers and sub-rulers according to their grade and number. Each level and sub level of the fallen angels are responsible for different areas of authority in the second heaven and rule over the earth through the minds of mankind.

PULLING DOWN STRONGHOLDS

Today the local church must set a pattern of activities that brings the power of the Holy Spirit. It all starts with prayer and worship. Then we must teach a gospel of power. I love to teach doctrine and theology, but it will always be proclaimed as having power.

> *Every kingdom divided against itself is brought to desolation, and every city or house divided against itself will not stand. If Satan casts out Satan, he is divided against himself. How then will his kingdom stand? Matthew 12:25–26*

A kingdom is an area or district ruled by a king. The definition says, it is a collective body of people and leaders that compose the domain of a king. However, prayer is a petition for God to reign, to manifest His kingly sovereignty and power, to put to flight every enemy of righteousness and of His divine rule, that God alone may be King over all the world. When the local church humbles themselves and prays, we are making or presenting a formal request to God for His sovereign rule and power to be exercised. We pray that God would put an end to every enemy of righteousness. At times, prophetic people may write down a formal prayer request and many people sign the request. This is the beginning of destroying a stronghold.

In this passage, Jesus stated very clearly that Satan has a kingdom and that they do not divide it. The definition of divided states that there is a collective body of evil spirits, a group, and leaders. Jesus divides Satan's kingdom into two groups: the demonic and the fallen angels. This organization, by definition, has social units and group associations. When searching the Bible Lexicon, a unit is a subdivision of a larger military grouping, each having a special function. When I am casting out demons, there is always a group and each individual demon has some common association with the demon God is judging. Let me use a military organization to help the reader. In the military there are platoons, divisions, companies, squadrons, regiments, brigades, battalions, not in military order but just listed. Can you see how organized the demonic kingdom is? The fallen organize the demons according to the fallen angelic structure. The fallen angels have set up the demonic realms according to how their own realms are arranged. There are many scriptures that verify my point. In Mark 1:24, the demon under God's judgment says, "Let us alone! What have we to do with You, Jesus of Nazareth?" Twice the one demon speaking for those in his unit or group! Then He went on to speak about the kingdom of God:

And if I cast out demons by Beelzebub, by whom do your sons cast them out? Therefore they shall be your judges. But if I cast out demons by the Spirit of God, surely the kingdom of God has come upon you. Matthew 12:27–28 NKJV

I believe that Satan particularly fears the ministry of deliverance for two reasons: First, because; It brings his invisible kingdom out into the open. He would much rather keep it secret. He would also like believers not to get involved in the pulling down of strongholds. This is how the army of Satan is defeated. Second, it shows the authority and power of God's kingdom over Satan's kingdom.

A king must have a kingdom or a realm to reign over! There are very few churches who have the authority to reign over a realm. Power churches can reign at their location but not affect the realm or region they are located in.

SPHERE OF AUTHORITY

And the angels who did not keep their proper domain, but left their own abode, He has reserved in everlasting chains under darkness for the judgment of the great day Jude 6 NKJV

Jude is speaking about the angels who fell. He says they did not keep their first estate. The word "estate" is the translation of archē (ἀρχή). The word means first, "beginning." When the definitions speak about beginnings, they refer to "first ones, preeminent ones, leaders," it means beginning, chief in order, time, place or rank; old or ancient; author, captain, prince. What is interesting about Jude 6 and authority? It means beginning; origin, a foundation, a source, at the beginning, ruler, power, office, elementary principles or principalities. The second meaning of archē (ἀρχή) is derived from the first, namely, "sovereignty, dominion, magistracy," the beginning or first place of power. The word is translated "principalities" in Ephesians 6:12, and refers to fallen angels there. Thus, this meaning of archē (ἀρχή) teaches that these angels left their original dignity and high positions. Archē (ἀρχή) is used in the Book of Enoch (12:4) of the Watchers (Angels) who have abandoned the high heaven and the holy eternal place and defiled themselves with women.

"The Watchers called me Enoch the scribe and said to me: Enoch, thou scribe of righteousness, go, declare to the Watchers of the heaven who have left the high heaven, the holy eternal place, and have defiled themselves with women, and have done as the children of earth do, and have taken unto themselves wives." Today in the terrestrial realm the fallen angels from the celestial realms exercise spheres of authority. They are environments over which a fallen angel exercises a controlling influence over the behavior of man. The ruling fallen angel enforces his reign by sub-ruling fallen angels. This is a multi-tiered kingdom.

There is one truth that we must embrace and understand: the healing ministry will never break the power of fallen angels within regions. I have come to understand that the reason people do not receive their healing is because a fallen angel has a legal right. The Church must learn how to subdue the fallen angels by having God send them down so we can turn the minds of mankind within a region toward Christ.

As I have pointed out through this book series, the unseen realm dictates and controls the seen realm. When the

Church fails to pray, decree and declare God's Word, evangelize, and operate in healing and deliverance, fallen angels establish authority and control over regions. They are areas owned or controlled by a fallen ruler who has a sphere of activity, manifesting his knowledge and power.

CHAPTER SIX

FALLEN ANGELS

The question is, did God place all the nations and their lands under the authority and power of fallen angels, but kept Israel and their land for His own? If the reader has listened to some expositors and programs concerning Israel and the land not having fallen angels in this evil Age, please stop. Israel is the apple of God's eye. The land is called the holy land, but Israel is estranged from God today. One day, the anti-christ will declare himself god in Israel. Since the fall of creation, Satan and his fallen angels have become the gods of this age, and that includes Israel.

As I lay a foundation for the explanation of Psalm 82 in the next chapter, we must look at the Hebrew word for "gods," elohim. It is not a metaphor, and it is not the worship of more than one god. It is a reference to created divine beings that we sometimes refer to as "angels." They are biblically referred to as "holy ones" (Deut 33:2-3; Heb 2:2), "host of heaven" (1 King 22:19-23) or "Sons of God" (Job 1:6; 38:7).

Whether we look at the Old Testament or the New Testament, anyone who refers to the false gods as being demonic spiritual powers has never encountered a fallen angel in combat. They also cannot explain scripturally who they are (Deut 32:17; Psa 106:37-38; 1 Cor 8:4-6; 10:18-20).

> *They provoked Him to jealousy with foreign gods;*
> *With abominations they provoked Him to anger.*
> *they sacrificed to demons, not to God, to gods they*
> *did not know, to new gods, new arrivals that your*
> *fathers did not fear. Deuteronomy 32:16-17 NKJV*

Israel was under the power and influence of fallen angelic rulers, and God's people worship them. How did they get Israel to do this? Deuteronomy says they did it through demon possession. Fallen angels do not possess, demons are the ones who possess. Demons through human desires had Israel bowing down to their rulers, the fallen angels. Yes, you read that right. Through demon possession, Israel worshipped foreign, not just the ones over their land, but foreign fallen angels. Do you see the cosmic hierarchy here? What is the hierarchical structure here?

A structured organization of levels and grades over Israel and other nations according to numbers within a hierarchy who are well organized as a kingdom of four different dimensions in the second heaven. These different kinds of fallen angels within each of the four dimensions have descending orders of authorities and different rulers and sub-rulers according to their grade and number. These fallen angels are responsible for different nations and areas of authority in the second heaven and rule over the whole earth through the minds of mankind.

This is not just an interpretation or some unproven theory, but ten years of combat with the fallen angels, including Satan himself twice.

> *They sacrificed their sons and their daughters to false gods. They shed innocent blood, the blood of their sons and daughters, whom they sacrificed to the idols of Canaan, and the land was desecrated by their blood. Psalm 106:37-38 NKJV*

Here is a key for all deliverance ministers, Israel took part in the nine covenants of the occult (Dt.18:10-12). They sacrificed their children to the rulers and authorities over their cities and nation. Israel created blood covenants with the fallen angels establishing a generational covenant by giving their future generation to the fallen angels. What are we talking about? The people of God today must go through second heaven deliverance.

> *Therefore concerning the eating of things offered to idols, we know that an idol is nothing in the world, and that there is no other God but one. For even if*

there are so-called gods, whether in heaven or on
earth (as there are many gods and many lords),
yet for us there is one God, the Father, of whom
are all things, and we for Him; and one Lord
Jesus Christ, through whom are all things, and
through whom we live. 1 Corinthians 8:4-6 NKJV

Paul acknowledged that many people believed the so-called gods to be real. The gods Paul is talking about is listed in dimensions in Colossians 1:16. Paul says, food is not what condemns us, but the surrender to these fallen angels. Paul tells us where images or idols come from:

Therefore since we are God's offspring, we
should not think that the divine being is like
gold or silver or stone—an image made by
human design and skill. Acts 17:29 NIV

So then, being God's children, we should not think
that the Divine Nature (deity) is like gold or
silver or stone, an image formed by the art and
imagination or skill of man. Acts 17:29 AMP

Paul was in Athens and standing in the center of the Areopagus, he tells the people where idols come from. Paul says they come from strongholds within. This is how a stronghold is formed, from false imaginations or reasonings that formed thoughts (2Cor.10:3-6) and led a craftsman to form a piece of art to worship. Notice it was in the mind first. This is the work of the second heaven. The influence over the mind of the craftsman led him to surrender to the demonic inside and create an abomination. This might be a lot to take in, but this series is a record of thousands of encounters with fallen angels and demonic spirits. All I am doing is giving a written account of the Holy Spirit's work through me.

In 1 Corinthians 10:18-20, Paul warned the Corinthians to "flee from idolatry" (10:14), and he supported his command with the fact that participants in biblical sacrificial meals have spiritual communion with God and with one another (10:16–18). Paul's point is clear. If such communion takes place in biblical sacrificial meals, then in some sense it also takes place in pagan sacrificial meals.

Let the heavens praise your wonders, O Lord,
your faithfulness in the assembly of the holy ones!
For who in the skies can be compared to the Lord?
Who among the heavenly beings is like the Lord,
a God greatly to be feared in the council of the holy
ones, and awesome above all who are around him?
Psalm 89:5-7 ESV

The Psalmist uses heavens in the plural, and when I trace the definition through it speaks of more than one. Paul tells us that there are three heavens and then tells us there are four dimensions to the second heaven. The heavens are where the angels live, both good and evil. When I trace the word heaven through definition, it speaks of supernatural regions and then supernatural entities who have souls. What we cannot leave out is regions of punishment. When Paul speaks of the third heaven, he says it is the highest level of the supernatural regions. Jesus speaks of a place He called paradise. Paradise is a supernatural region that is secure and a walled garden full of delightful blessings and delicacies.

The holy ones the psalmist is talking about are the angels, both good and bad. Then he mentions skies, the regions above the earth from beyond where birds fly to the farthest star and is associated with the abode of angels. There are divine beings or sons of God who dwell far above the earth's atmosphere yet have supernatural extension into the earth. There are many regions, just as there are different dimensions. The sky in scripture is also understood as the realm where evil spirits dwell and come from to exercise their influence. The definition speaks of the celestial and terrestrial realms.

COMING WAR

Let us look at Revelation 9:1-12,

> *And the fifth angel blew his trumpet, and I saw a star fallen from heaven to earth, and he was given the key to the shaft of the bottomless pit. He opened the shaft of the bottomless pit, and from the shaft rose smoke like the smoke of a great furnace, and the sun and the air were darkened with the smoke from the shaft. Then from the smoke came locusts on the earth, and they were given power like the power of scorpions of the earth. They were told not to harm the grass of the earth or any green plant or*

any tree, but only those people who do not have the seal of God on their foreheads. They were allowed to torment them for five months, but not to kill them, and their torment was like the torment of a scorpion when it stings someone. And in those days people will seek death and will not find it. They will long to die, but death will flee from them.

In appearance the locusts were like horses prepared for battle: on their heads were what looked like crowns of gold; their faces were like human faces, their hair like women's hair, and their teeth like lions' teeth; they had breastplates like breastplates of iron, and the noise of their wings was like the noise of many chariots with horses rushing into battle. They have tails and stings like scorpions, and their power to hurt people for five months is in their tails. They have as king over them the angel of the bottomless pit. His name in Hebrew is Abaddon, and in Greek he is called Apollyon.

I am now giving the reader a glimpse into a future book about the coming war between God's angels with the Church verses Satan's angels, demons, and evil, wicked people.

Our scripture addresses a real war in a real spiritual world that eventually invades our world spiritually and physically. The imagery is terrifying as the spiritual realm invades the physical world where fallen angels and demons are let loose to bring devastation, destruction, and death. John's vision gives us a future look into the armies of darkness and the battle that awaits the Church. Through this book series and my battles with fallen angels, God is now putting in print what will be the foundation for the coming war. We can better understand how fallen angels operate and the wickedness that is tormenting mankind today.

John saw a star, a fallen angelic being that had fallen from heaven to the earth; and the key of the bottomless pit (abyss) was given to him. In Revelation, falling stars or lightning symbolized falling members of the heavenly host, whether Satan himself (Lk 10:18), Wormwood (Rev 8:10) or the nameless fallen angel who releases the scorpion armies from the bottomless pit (Rev 9:1). They are allowed to inflict mankind with mental and physical diseases that cause man to desire death. This in a measure is happening today.

Most believe that the army released is demonic, but who is their leader? It is my combat experience and my theology that states: the army is both demonic spirits and fallen angels. Remember the Watchers or fallen angels of the heavens who have left the high heaven, the holy eternal place, and have defiled themselves with women, and what they have done to the children of earth, still influence this evil Age. This war will be cosmic and unknown in number, engaging all of God's angels and all the armies of Satan. The scripture states, the angel of the abyss (the bottomless pit); in Hebrew his name is Abaddon (destruction), and in Greek he is called Apollyon (destroyer-king), will be one of the chief leaders. I have faced him in combat. If God has called us to face them now, what will it be like in the future.

What did God do in Christ Jesus? He disarmed the rulers and authorities having triumphed over them through the cross. God through Christ stripped the fallen angels of their authority and power against those who are in Christ Jesus. Therefore, those who take on these rulers and authorities can also defeat them. We cannot take away the weapons of the fallen angels or their foot soldiers, the demonic, if we do not know what those weapons are. It was the fallen angels who taught mankind unrighteousness and ungodliness. God has created and given to man the power of understanding the word of wisdom, so has God created the Church and given us the power of reprimanding the Watchers, the children of heaven or the fallen angels. How is this done through "it is written"?

GOD JUDGES

There are those who believe the fallen angel's punishment is loss of both their immortality and their inheritance of nations at Babel. They will argue that it accomplished this in the first century comprising events of Messiah's death, resurrection, ascension and arrival of God's kingdom. We know that all created beings will live forever; it is the place in which created beings will live, the Age to Come or pits of darkness. Jesus' death and resurrection dealt the kingdom of darkness their first of three blows. The second will occur when Jesus institutes the Millennium. The third, a fatal blow, will come when Christ reigns as King until He has put all His enemies under His feet, the last enemy to be abolished and put to an end is death.

> *It was also about these that Enoch, the seventh*
> *from Adam, prophesied, saying, "Behold, the*
> *Lord comes with ten thousands of his holy ones,*
> *15 to execute judgment on all and to convict*
> *all the ungodly of all their deeds of ungodliness*
> *that they have committed in such an ungodly*
> *way, and of all the harsh things that ungod-*
> *ly sinners have spoken against him." [This is*
> *quoted from 1Enoch 1:9].Jude 14,15 ESV*

When theologians write about scriptures like this, they so mislead the body of Christ. This scripture is so easily exampled if we have encountered fallen angels and defeated them in combat. They take Jude 6-7 and 1Peter 3:18 and draw from 1Enoch to describe the sin of the Watchers before the Flood and their punishment of being chained in Tartarus "until the judgment of the great day." These theologians believe that the fallen angels (Watchers) are chained in Tartarus now; it is not so. They are all over the second heaven and ruling through the minds of man today. Tartarus is the place the Church sends them through combat encounters. It is an awesome sight to see as they scream when the eternal chains of darkness are placed on them. Once they are in chains and we the Church declare Psalm 82 over them the fallen cry out even louder as the enforcement of God's judgment goes into action.

> *Then I saw a great white throne and Him who sat*
> *on it, from whose face the earth and the heaven fled*

> *away. And there was found no place for them. And
> I saw the dead, small and great, standing before
> God, and books were opened. And another book
> was opened, which is the Book of Life. And the
> dead were judged according to their works, by
> the things which were written in the books. The
> sea gave up the dead who were in it, and Death
> and Hades delivered up the dead who were in
> them. And they were judged, each one according
> to his works. Then Death and Hades were cast
> into the lake of fire. This is the second death. And
> anyone not found written in the Book of Life was
> cast into the lake of fire. Rev. 20:11–15 NKJV*

The Lord said to Raphael: 'Bind Azâzêl hand and foot, and cast him into the darkness: and make an opening in the desert, which is in Dûdâêl, and cast him therein. And place upon him rough and jagged rocks, and cover him with darkness, and let him abide there forever, and cover his face that he may not see light. And on the day of the great judgment he shall be cast into the fire. 1 Enoch 10:1-7

> *For if God did not spare angels when they
> sinned, but cast them into hell and commit-
> ted them to chains of gloomy darkness to be
> kept until the judgment. 2 Peter 2:4 NKJV*

Wait for it! When I take the book of Revelation, Enoch, and Peter along with second heaven deliverance, Peter is writing about where to send the fallen angels and how to do it.

And to Michael God said, "Make known to Semyaza and the others who are with him, who fornicated with the women, that they will die together with them in all their defilement. And when they and all their children have battled with each other, and when they have seen the destruction of their beloved ones, bind them for seventy generations underneath the rocks of the ground until the day of their judgment and of their consummation, until the eternal judgment is concluded. In those days they will lead them into the bottom of the fire—and in torment—in the prison (where) they will be locked up forever. And at the time when they will burn and die, those who collaborated with them will be bound together with them from henceforth unto the end of (all) generations. And destroy all the souls of pleasure and the children of the Watchers, for they have done injustice to man, 1 Enoch 10:11-15.

Where are the Watchers, who declare their name to me as the fallen (category), bound today until all is completed, in darkness? To those who have never battled a fallen angel who wears the name of Christ Jesus or any other cosmic name, cannot rightly see that Jude and Peter write in the past, present, and future; just like the Holy Spirit their author.

Then Michael, Raphael, Gabriel, and Phanuel themselves shall seize [the sinful Watchers] on that great day of judgment and cast them into the furnace (of fire) that is burning that day, so that the Lord of the Spirits may take vengeance on them, 1 Enoch 54:6.

> *The Son of Man will send his angels, and they*
> *will gather out of his kingdom all causes of sin*
> *and all law-breakers, and throw them into the*
> *fiery furnace. In that place there will be weeping*
> *and gnashing of teeth. Matthew 13:41–42*

The parable seems to refer to all sinners, and to conclude that law-breaking angels who cause sin will be included in that fiery judgment. Especially since 1Enoch describes a furnace of fire for the Watchers. Whose kingdom is it today, Jesus'? Who will suffer the fiery furnace, all causes of sin and lawlessness?

Many other scriptures teach this final judgment. Paul tells the Greek philosophers in Athens that God now commands all men everywhere to repent, because he has fixed a day on which he will judge the world in righteousness by a man whom he has appointed, and of this he has given assurance to all men by raising him from the dead (Acts 17:30–31). Likewise, Paul talks about "the day of wrath when God's righteous judgment will be revealed" (Rom. 2:5). Other passages speak clearly of a coming day of judgment (see Matt. 10:15; 11:22, 24; 12:36; 25:31–46; 1 Cor. 4:5; Heb. 6:2; 2 Peter 2:4; Jude 6;).

Here is my point, God is judging today, tomorrow, and until the end of this evil Age. The fallen angelic realms, the demonic realms, and all the generations that will live on this earth are being judged everyday. God is either judging condemnation or He is judging on our behalf in righteousness.

CHAPTER SEVEN
PSALM 82

God has taken his place in the divine council;
in the midst of the gods he holds judgment:
"How long will you judge unjustly
and show partiality to the wicked? Selah

Give justice to the weak and the fatherless;
maintain the right of the afflicted
and the destitute.
Rescue the weak and the needy;
deliver them from the hand of the wicked."
They have neither knowledge nor understanding,
they walk about in darkness;
all the foundations of the earth are shaken.

I said, "You are gods,

sons of the Most High, all of you;
nevertheless, like men you shall die,
and fall like any prince."
Arise, O God, judge the earth;
for you shall inherit all the nations
Psalm 82:1-8,

It is clear that the psalmist Asaph is addressing God in prayer. The prayer is asking God to take action according to the evil of the fallen angels. The original Hebrew word translated "gods" is elohim, and it refers to any resident of the spirit world. Elohim does not refer to a specific set of abilities but distinguishes God from all other spirit beings. Asaph states that through prayer the Church can ask God to hold court. Like Asaph, we can ask God to have territorial fallen angels and fallen angels over bloodlines appear or to go up before God's court. While "the divine assembly" is more literally "the assembly of 'ēl," "God" and "gods" both translate the word 'ĕlōhîm. But at its first occurrence 'ĕlōhîm governs a singular verb and clearly refers to God while at the second "in the midst of 'ĕlōhîm" is clearly plural, addressing angelic realms. The Creator of the universe appears in the heavenly courtroom and stands in position as a judge. From the definition all in the courtroom stand in respect before God as He presents Himself.

God "presides" (niṣṣāb ; cf. Isa 3:13; Am 7:7; 9:1) as the Great Judge. God assembles the "gods" together for judgment in "the assembly of El" (NIV, "the great assembly"). The assembly of El is a borrowed phrase from Canaanite mythology, according to which El, the chief of the pantheon, assembled the gods in a divine council. God takes His stand in the position of authority as the One in charge and who is responsible as law giver in the great assembly of the gods or angelic beings. Remember, in my book series, I commented on how the fallen angelic majesties gather together in counsel to rule over regions. Now God is calling those counsels before His court.

In Psalm 29:1 says, "Ascribe to the Lord, O heavenly beings, ascribe to the Lord glory and strength." The gods are commanded to worship God their creator as Psalm 148:1-5 speaks of. When we examine verse one, it refers to the stance taken by a supreme ruler to receive the acknowledgment of his lordship in his court, and to address the accused by stating charges and to pronounce sentence. To stand means to attend or officially manage and to sort out. The God of the Bible is officiating a court case. He is there to oppose His enemies and to bring the fallen angels to court for wrong doing. We can see that it is God who judges the fallen angels.

In verse two, God has the authority and power to call the fallen angels over nations to account. The question how long in verse two does not seek an answer, however, but introduces a complaint and a demand that the unjust and evil activities of the fallen angels be punished for disobeying God's laws. The gods, administrators of God have imposed crooked and devious schemes of injustice on humanity, showing favoritism to the wicked and ignoring the pleas of the righteous for help. Therefore, Asaph has the right in prayer to come before God and ask Him to accuse or bring charges against the fallen for their defense of those who are unjust, perverse or showing partiality to the wicked.

The person who has the approval to operate in God's courts, appears in prayer and humility and pleads his case that the lawlessness of the fallen angels stop, cease immediately. In today's language, the person whom God has appointed to operate in His court is to lead people in a declaration prayer. This criminal court proceeding concerns two things. One, the sins mankind has committed within that territory from the beginning and second, the lawlessness of the kingdom of darkness in that region. Asaph calls for both an indictment and a command that the gods cease judging unjustly. To judge in the spirit realm for the wicked.

These angels at one time represented God and held different level judgeships. Now Asaph is prayerfully asking that God recall their commission and to remove them from their magistrate. The prayer is for God to review these officers who judge over nations and who were to administer the law of God.

Within each region, whether a nation, state, county, city or zip code, Asaph is saying that we are to bring a court case against the fallen angel's jurisdiction for their continual influence and approval of injustice. In volume one of "Exploring Secrets of the Heavenly Realms", the chapter on territorial spirits, we must find out if this is a civil or criminal trial. If the trial is criminal, it is then officiated and judged according to the sins in our bloodline, and the sins of the population within that district. If the trial is civil, the court case will be personal sins and bloodline transgressions.

Verse three reveals a powerful prayer and a major revelation for God's people. God actively desires to intervene in the interest of powerless people who cannot defend their rights because of the sin nature. As I have written before, the sin nature is the satanic principle. The sinful nature of humanity is the foundation and the system in which the fallen angels accuse and operate in mankind. Because this nature is of Satan, our beliefs, attitudes, and behavior desire control. Therefore, a stronghold exhibits itself in three parts. The Bible teaches that every lie forms a stronghold foundation. Second, that lie calls for a chain of reasonings which then caps off the stronghold by thoughts that try to convince.

Asaph prays, give justice or vindicate, which is to hear and be the judge of a legal case. The indictment of the fallen angels is because they are a reminder of the original commission to the gods: to provide for those who cannot help themselves, the weak, fatherless, poor, oppressed, and needy. The fallen angels are now reminded in Asaph's prayer, this is what the 'gods' should have done.

We now come to verse four! The fallen angels are to be brought to court because they have failed to act on behalf of the needy and weak. They have weakened mankind and are in need of help because of the sinful nature. Asaph's prayer is for God to do justice by delivering mankind who seeks Him. Man is like a child who does not have a father to teach and guide. Asaph states in verse four for God to rescue man out of the hand of the fallen angels. Mankind needs to be delivered from fallen angles.

It was the original duty of judges or the fallen angels to protect those who are powerless to defend themselves. But that obligation was forsaken here. In the original commission before the fallen angels abandoned heaven, God said to them, "Defend the cause of the weak and fatherless from the injustices they face." They should protect the innocent from the injustices of evil men who drag them into court. Maintain the rights of the poor and oppressed from those who take advantage of them; God demanded. Rescue the weak and needy from being exploited by the wicked.

Asaph uses the word rescue, which is a deliverance term that asks for God to help in the recovery of the human identity and the loss of God's divine preservation because of the fall. Asaph is praying that the influence and authority of the fallen angels which mankind lives under be removed. The prayer is a request to preserve life and the sustenance that sustains life, both physically and spiritually.

This psalm helps us understand why the wicked prosper, the elohim or the fallen angels abuse their power and reward evil. They are the ones who influenced evil in the garden and are using their commission or anointing to spread evil throughout this evil Age.

This is a formal charge by God in verse five of the gods, the fallen angel's true character as the verse describes. Their disobedience to the sovereign Lord has caused them to act foolishly. The New Testament refers to these rulers as a spiritual power in the heavenly places. Asaph is talking about the fallen angels or majesties who govern over humanity and exercise authority over them through wickedness. The definitions speak to the fallen angels as the original law breakers within their realms. These fallen angels were to officiate as God's servants the laws and precepts of God. They were to exercise God's authority through their commission.

When the psalmist says, they know nothing; they understand nothing; he is referring to their eyes being plastered over so they cannot see, and their minds closed so they cannot understand. This word plastered is a very strong word that means being very drunk with darkness. He also says, the fallen angels have darkened their intelligence and their reasoning has brought about God's judgment. The fallen angel's opinions and way of thinking desires evil all the time. Asaph used the word darkness or falsity to describe their knowledge.

The fallen angels walking about is the territory they oversee and their influence evil. God says it is impossible for such gods or fallen angels to know, understand, have the ability, to see what is right. Because of the influence of fallen angels and demon possession, lawlessness has affected the ground, territory, country, and the earth. Asaph reveals, as lawlessness spreads the universe becomes defiled or is stained with sin and is impure ritually and morally. Jeremiah 3:1 says the same thing.

When injustice and perversity have their way in the world, it shakes the spiritual and moral world order and comes under the threat of collapse. Asaph says the foundations or the lower earthly realm (the terrestrial realm where humanity dwells and at one time had authority) is defiled. The Psalm points too, if the gods had their way, the fallen would destroy the universe in a short time.

So it will happen in that day
That the Lord will visit and punish the host (fallen
angels) of heaven on high,
And the kings of the earth on the earth.
Isaiah 24:21 AMP

What day is Isaiah talking about, the day Christ came to earth, and His return to earth? When Jesus came through the incarnation, He came as the last Adam and the Son of God. He stripped the kingdom of darkness of its authority and power. Therefore, as man exercises Christ's reign, the kingdom of light overtakes the darkness. Christ Jesus has given the Church the ability to drive out or expel demons spirits and to incarcerate the fallen angels today. Jesus will finish the job when He turns the Kingdom of God over to God the Father. We also know that there will be a one thousand year imprisonment of the kingdom of darkness at the Millennium.

In verse seven, God pronounces a judgment on the fallen angels and their demons. He calls them gods or supernatural beings who were before the creation of the world and rulers over the universe. God also calls the fallen His sons or children, and it refers to a collective. When Asaph prophesies their death, the definition alludes to the state of life they now have with the attributes and function necessary to sustain that life.

God said, you are gods [since you judge on My behalf, as My representatives]; all of you are children of the Most High, but you shall die as men and fall as one of the princes. To fall as one of the princes is to fall like mankind and to die for it. The beginning of the judgment finishes this powerful Psalm. The judgement against the fallen is because they have violated their purpose and mission to which God called them. But now God is judging them for their stupidity and rebellion. This is a powerful thing to watch, as they are chained with eternal chains of darkness and sentenced to tartaros.

CHAPTER EIGHT

SUPERNATURAL KEYS

One of the major keys to the supernatural for me has been the study of the Holy Spirit's movements. I have spent countless hours reading scriptures, doing word definitions, and researching authors on the subjects of how the Holy Spirit does things. Therefore, let us look at the difference between oppression and possession or demonization. Oppression is nothing more than mental torment because of demon possession. Let's define oppression according to Acts 10:38, which says, "how God anointed Jesus of Nazareth with the Holy Spirit and with great power; and He went around doing good and healing all who were oppressed by the devil, because God was with Him." (AMP) Oppression is to have or exercise power over or to exercise harsh control over one. Oppression is that overwhelming feeling to sin until the person gives in and sins. It means to use one's power against another. Evil spirits use our mental choices, known as free will, against us. It also means to conquer and to be enslaved, even to be treated as a slave. This is mental torment and possession! Oppression originates in the mind as the body is feeling the impulse. Therefore, since the body feels the desire to sin revealing demonization, then mental oppression is the giving over of the freedom of choice. Each time someone chooses sin, that piece of their will stays captive until they can no longer say NO!

What does that spiritually mean to use one's power against another? It means that evil is to put such pressure through the sinful nature that the person uses the power of free will to choose evil, invoking a contract or marriage with those evil spirits. To be oppressed is to be subdued. Evil spirits seek to dominate the will of humanity. Evil spirits tempt, but it is the free choice of the person who decides freedom or demonization. The kingdom of darkness tempts mankind through the sinful nature, testing for willful surrender, creating a legal right through contract.

> *Do not love the world [of sin that opposes God and His precepts], nor the things that are in the world. If anyone loves the world, the love of the Father is not in him. 16 For all that is in the world—the lust and sensual craving of the flesh and the lust and longing of the eyes and the boastful pride of life [pretentious confidence in one's resources or in the stability of earthly things]—these do not come from the Father, but are from the world. 17 The*

world is passing away, and with it its lusts [the
shameful pursuits and ungodly longings]; but
the one who does the will of God and carries out
His purposes lives forever. 1 John 2:15-17 AMP

On July 7, 2019, I had a woman come to me for help. All she could say is, pastor, I feel like running to the world. The Holy Spirit instantly spoke to me 1 John 2:15-17. I knew this exorcism would have to do with the love of the world. She was in our foundations class we call first principals. Her condition started with cloudiness, confusion, and a headache. She could not focus and receive the word that was being spoken in first principals. She was feeling a lot of pressure in her head and wanted to run out of the church because she didn't feel safe. She felt scared and her mind wanted to run to evil like she needed it, and even her body felt like it was coming down with the flu.

This was a classic case of inner healing, demonic possession, all under the control of a fallen angel whose name is "love of the world." We have come to understand from the book series, "Exploring Secrets of the Heavenly Realms," that fallen angels do not have names like demons. Can you see the possession or demonization and the oppression of the mind by the fallen angel? Her condition started with the appearance of the fallen angel through the manifestation of mental cloudiness, confusion or having a hard time putting thoughts together and a headache. Notice how her focus was off, not being able to receive the foundations of the Word of God. The fallen angel called the "love of the world" came down on his own authority to block her understanding of the Word of God. We see pictures like this in the book of Acts.

Second, notice how she was fearful and did not feel safe indicting this was an inner healing issue. We see the demonization in two manifestations: she felt in her mind, which reveals possession in the body, and her body felt flu like systems. It was all under the control of the fallen angel "love of the world." I first ministered to the inner healing aspect, healing the brokenhearted. Afterwards, I then asked God in Jesus' name for the judgment of the "love of the world." I have had many second heaven deliverances, so I did not go after the demon first, understanding the demon was probably protected by the fallen angel.

I will now give the reader her word by word account as God judged the fallen angel "love of the world" according to the work of Christ Jesus on the cross.

"My head started to shake and I could feel all the evil thoughts being pulled out of my mind. I could see a black web as my head was shaking. A web of lies. I cried because I knew Jesus was taking the torment and I was so relieved. When I started to cry I knew I was going to be delivered and was being delivered from something that had a hold of my mind all my life. I felt immediate relief afterwards and my head was relieved of confusion, pressure and anxiety. I had peace. It's hard to explain exactly. But I know I felt Jesus like never before and I cried because I was so thankful with everything in me that He was taking this web of lies out of my mind that had been there since a child or even birth."

As stated in my books, her head started to shake, this does not happen all the time. Then all the evil thoughts were pulled out of her mind; this is a second heaven deliverance. The believer who is going though second heaven deliverance feels in the mind the extraction or the drawing out of lies and unbeliefs. She had been seeking freedom and had some inner healing and deliverance sessions before. It was the foundations of the faith that the fallen angel "love of the world" did not want her to understand. Whether the extraction is mentally painful, the squeezing out of the fallen angel from the mind or a manifestation, the mind becomes free when the fallen pull out. The squeezing out or the pressing out of the mind can be painful as the fallen angel fights to stay in control of the mind. She knew in her mind that Jesus was setting her free and she stayed in agreement by wanting her freedom. The result was, "love of the world" pulled out and left, then she started to cough and vomit, demons coming out.

We see how the demonic structure serves and works for the fallen angels. This second heaven deliverance was a textbook deliverance from fallen angels.

STRONGHOLDS

There are three sides to a stronghold described by Paul in 2 Corinthians 10:3-6. The first side or foundation of a stronghold is knowledge. So the first side or foundation of a demonic or a fallen angel stronghold is false knowledge or belief in a lie. The second side or middle foundation is imaginations or arguments, reasonings of the mind. The final side or the top of the foundation is thoughts.

> *For though we walk in the flesh, we do not war according to the flesh. For the weapons of our warfare are not carnal but mighty in God for pulling down strongholds, casting down arguments and every high thing that exalts itself against the knowledge of God, bringing every thought into captivity to the obedience of Christ, and being ready to punish all disobedience when your obedience is fulfilled. 2 Corinthians 10:3-6 NKJV*

We could translate verse three as follows: "For even though we are living in the world, we do not wage war in a worldly manner." As believers, we live in this temporal evil Age and we also live now from the Age to come. This could not be pictured more clearly. Paul is revealing two worlds now, the kingdom of darkness and the Kingdom of Light. And God has "blessed us in Christ with every spiritual blessing in the heavenly places" (Ephesians 1:3). Both the seating and blessing are now, in the present, though the full realization will happen at Christ's return.

The fallen angel called "love of the world" had a ruling influence over her mind, giving her the controlling thoughts of returning to a worldly lifestyle. It was the Word of God that brought about the feelings and her condition. Notice how she described her body as having flu-like symptoms. This was not a spirit of infirmity, but the fallen angel exercising control of the mind and ordering the demonic to make the body feel the condition. The conditions she felt in her body were because of demonization. The headache, mental cloudiness, her ears being clogged, and confusion because of having a hard time putting thoughts together was from the fallen angel. The demons under the orders of "love of the world" made the body feel weak, tired, even lethargic. Her body was being drained of physical strength, and her nervousness was because of the alter personalities feeling the presence of the fallen angel.

This is what she said after the second heaven deliverance. "I was feeling physically ill and mentally drained. It felt like there was a blockage in my mind. I couldn't pay attention or receive what was being taught in the first principles class." Now most believers would excuse themselves from the class saying they are feeling sick and tried.

The Wuest Greek New Testament says, the word "world" here are kosmos (κοσμος) which in its use here is defined by Vincent: The sum-total of human life in the ordered world, considered apart from, alienated from, and hostile to God, and of the earthly things which seduce from God. The fallen angel, "love of the world" was causing this woman to have great affections or a caring desire for the world hostile to God. When the definition from the Bible Lexicon talks about caring, it speaks of loyalty toward the world. Therefore, this is what the fallen angel was demanding from this woman. The root definition for love is to feel emotion. Can you see how this woman was manifesting the definition? The fallen angel was demanding her loyalty and her affections for him. He would do whatever it took to separate her from the Word of God and God's desires, that is, to study His foundations.

Kenneth Wuest says, "The kosmos (Κοσμος) refers to an ordered system. Here it is the ordered system of which Satan is the head, his fallen angels and demons are his emissaries, and the unsaved of the human race are his subjects, together with those purposes, pursuits, pleasures, practices, and places where God is not wanted." However, this woman was born again and had received the baptism of the Holy Spirit. She had gone through several demonic deliverances, but was still struggling with desires for the world. Therefore, the world could pull on both the unsaved and the saved. She belonged to Jesus spiritually, but parts of her mind and body belonged to the gods of this evil Age. Look closely at what the Apostle John writes. "If anyone loves the world, the love of the Father is not in him." The word anyone covers everyone!

What we must conclude from the freedom Jesus gave to this woman is that evil is not something but someone. This is a vital key in understanding spiritual warfare. Another powerful point is that believers can be spiritually set free, but mentally and physically belong to the gods of this evil Age.

PERILOUS TIMES

The Apostle Paul tells Timothy, that in the last days dangerous times [of great stress and trouble] will come [difficult days that will be hard to bear]. Paul is saying that darkness will continue to increase, dominated by fallen angels who will intensify and grow evil, sinfulness, and the ignorance of Christ Jesus in the world. These different spheres of authority are influenced and increasingly growing. In second Timothy 3:1-5, Paul gave us a very vivid description of the degeneration of human character that will mark the close of this age. He also uses the Greek word from Matthew 8:28 concerning the demonic of Gadara. Paul is pointing to a highly demonized society that will be very dangerous to live in and difficult to deal with.

It is a very dangerous situation to have powerful and active enemies working against you and not even know that you have those enemies. As Christians, the enemies we face are not persons of flesh and blood; they are invisible spirit beings. The themes we have been dealing with in this book series concern matters that are not discerned by human senses. The Bible speaks about things that "eye has not seen, nor ear heard, nor have entered into the heart of man" (1 Corinthians 2:9). These things are invisible and spiritual. We only understand them through the Scriptures. There is no other source of reliable information.

Paul said that the things that are seen are short lived; The things that are not seen are eternal. Therefore, our sensory world is passing away and only partly real because it does not endure. (See 2 Corinthians 4:18). But the spiritual world that we cannot see, that we cannot perceive with our senses, is the true reality.

God desires to give us wisdom and revelation as we open our hearts to His Word, because we are dealing with matters known only through scriptural revelation as combat encounters take place. Revelation without manifestation is only a dream. What we are dealing with are two opposing kingdoms at war with one another. They are invisible spiritual kingdoms. One is the kingdom of God and the other is the kingdom of Satan.

Isaiah 14 introduces us to a being called Lucifer. In its Latin root, the word Lucifer means "the one who brings light." The word arch, from its Greek root, means "ruling." The same word occurs in the word archbishop, a bishop who rules other bishops. Thus, an archangel is an angel who rules other angels. For example, in one of my previous books, I wrote about the fallen angel called "the light bearer." In second heaven deliverance, the fallen give their function and not their name. This is my experience as of July 2019.

Christ has clearly won the victory. However, He leaves it to us to enforce that victory. It is very important that we understand this. If we had to win the victory, we could never do it. In Matthew 28:18, Jesus says all authority in heaven and on earth has been given to me. Therefore, go and make disciples of all nations. The mission is clear; we have to exercise Jesus' authority. In a sense, His authority is completely ineffective until we exercise it. To exercise authority with power, we must be fully trained.

Look how Paul brings the fallen angels out into the open

from scripture. For though we walk in the flesh, we do not war according to the flesh (2 Corinthians 10:3). Paul said that we live in physical bodies and that it involves us in a war. But the war is not in the physical realm. If the war is not in the physical realm, it must be in the spiritual. For the weapons of our warfare are not carnal but mighty in God for pulling down strongholds [or fortresses], casting down arguments and every high thing that exalts itself against the knowledge of God, bringing every thought into captivity to the obedience of Christ (vv. 4,5). Where the New King James Version says "arguments," other versions say "reasonings" (Young's Literal Translation) or "speculations" (NAS). We also find the words knowledge and thought used in this verse. If we examine those five words—arguments, reasonings, speculations, knowledge, and thought—we recognize they all belong to the same realm: the mind. Paul reveals that our minds need to be delivered from lies, unbelief, and mindsets that exalt themselves against the Word of God.

The battlefield is the mind. That is where the battle is fought. Anyone who has tried to live the Christian life has discovered this. Therefore, the battle is with the fallen angels who have a controlling influence over the mind through the sinful nature. In our scripture verses (2 Corinthians 10:3-5) most writers leave out the power verse. The power verse is verse 6, being ready to punish all disobedience when your obedience is fulfilled. God stands ready to punish the fallen angels once we have met the conditions, that is obedience.

THE POWER OF THE WORD OF GOD

I would like to look at a few scriptures that reveal the power of the Word of God.

> *By the word of the Lord the heavens were made,*
> *And by the breath of His mouth all their host.*
> *Psalm 33:6 NASB*

The single noun heaven emphasizes its overall unity. Here in this Psalm, we see the plural form which suggests several locations all combined under the heading heaven. We also know that these places may be given over at various times to different beings and different activities. In the New Testament, heaven is the abode of God and his angels. The Son descended from heaven, ascended to it, and will return from it. The Holy Spirit also descended from heaven at Jesus' baptism and at Pentecost (cf. 1 Pet. 1:12). As in the Old Testament, 'heaven' often means God himself, hence Matthew's 'kingdom of heaven' and the prodigal son's sin 'against heaven'.

Let us look at the Hebrew word for breath and its translation, spirit. What the psalmist is saying, all creation took place through two agents: the Word of God and the Spirit of God. Everything that has ever existed or will ever exist owes its origin to two powerful forces, the Word of God and the Spirit of God. From the pattern set, the Word of God and the Spirit of God must work together. How do we speak? We release breath out of our mouth as we speak. So we learn a basic truth; we cannot speak without breathing. Therefore, we have a likeness with God. Every time God speaks, He releases His breath or His Spirit. Every time we speak, we release the Holy Spirit or spirits from the kingdom of darkness. Now let us look at a very powerful scripture in 2 Peter 3 and we will see that the Word of God creates, the Word maintains, the Word abolishes.

For when they maintain this, it escapes their notice that by the word of God the heavens existed long ago and the earth was formed out of water and by water, 6 through which the world at that time was destroyed, being flooded with water. 7 But by His word the present heavens and earth are being reserved for fire, kept for the day of judgment and destruction of ungodly men. 2 Peter 3:5-6 NASB

By the Word of God the heavens were brought into being; by the Word of God they are maintained in being, and by the Word of God, when God's time comes, they will pass away. So we see that the Word of God creates, maintains, and abolishes.

"For as the rain and snow come down from heaven,
And do not return there
without watering the earth,
Making it bear and sprout,
And providing seed to the
sower and bread to the eater,
11 So will My word be which goes out of My mouth;
It will not return to Me void (useless, without
result),

Without accomplishing what I desire,
And without succeeding in the matter for which I
sent it.
Isaiah 55:10-11 AMP

Just as the Word had to come out of God's mouth, the Word must come out of our mouth. Let me give the reader an example. When God gives me a word of knowledge concerning healing, and the person does not get healed, I then turn to deliverance and cast out the spirit of infirmity; whatever the name of the sickness. The same principle is true when dealing with fallen angels. In over one thousand power encounters, God has always had me say, "it is written." When I speak the Word of God to the fallen, the Word of God judges them for their guilt.

It has become evident to me, the believer who doubts the power of the Word of God or who is not constantly changed by the Word's power, requires second heaven deliverance and the freedom of the mind.

I believe we can go a little deeper now! In this section of the chapter, we must learn to speak God's Word and have that Word empowered by the Holy Spirit.

Who also made us adequate as servants
of a new covenant, not of the letter but of
the Spirit; for the letter kills, but the Spir-
it gives life. 2 Corinthians 3:6 NASB

Paul says the letter kills! Therefore, God's Word without

the empowering work of the Holy Spirit kills because it is the Holy Spirit that provides the Word of God authority and power that creates life. When Jesus began to teach, He was releasing words that had authority and power. What was the work of the Holy Spirit through the words of Jesus? He was imparting knowledge that brought about skills; the experiences would produce a change in the course of this evil Age.

MAKING THE WORD OF GOD EFFECTIVE

We will now look at some practical ways in which we can make the Word of God effective by proclaiming "it is written." We must release the Word of God into every situation, more so when we are operating in the supernatural. Speaking the Word of God takes boldness and confidence; It is not for the timid. We are to speak in faith and that takes a transform mind who believes. We need to say to ourselves, if I proclaim "it is written" with a believing heart and my breath goes forth, it is just as if God had said it and His Spirit went forth to make it effective. Can we believe the Word of God can be just as effective when we say it, just like God. When we proclaim "it is written" through the Holy Spirit, that same power goes forth.

When Moses had his God encounter on mount Sinai, he became frightened and threw his rod down on the ground and it became a snake which caused him to run from it. Before we can be effective in proclaiming "it is written" we must respect our adversary and be fully equipped. Another powerful truth is that we must learn to be afraid of the Word of God. We would be wise if we could learn to tremble at the Word of God.

> *"Heaven is My throne,*
> *And earth is My footstool.*
> *Where is the house that you will build Me?*
> *And where is the place of My rest?*
> *For all those things My hand has made,*
> *And all those things exist,"*
> *Says the Lord.*
> *"But on this one will I look:*
> *On him who is poor and of a contrite spirit,*
> *And who trembles at My word.*
> *Isaiah 66:1-2 NKJV*

The Lord says, there is nothing we can build Him or there is nothing we can use of this earth to give to God, but we recognize one fact that impresses God. There is one thing that attracts God's favor or causes God to look: one translation says respect. God will respect the one who is poor and of a contrite spirit and who trembles at His Word. I would suggest to the reader, until we learn to tremble at God's Word, we truly cannot be humble and willing to be broken. We should ask ourselves, what are we willing to go through in this life, to honor and respectfully fear God's Word. Until we can proclaim "it is written" in confidence, fearfully or in awe of God's Word, we will not see much power.

There is far too little fear of the Word of God in the Church today. We have become too familiar with it. We quote it or listen to it preached, but we do not show real reverence for God's Word. How can a believer expect to see the power of God's Word, if that believer will not obey it. There is no honor or fear of God in that believer. When God has me say in Jesus' name, "it is written" to the fallen angels, I see instant power and authority unto judgement. If the angelic realm fears God's Word, how about us who were created a little lower than the angels.

I will close this chapter out with two reasons why we should tremble at the Word of God.

> *If anyone hears My sayings and does not keep them, I do not judge him; for I did not come to judge the world, but to save the world. He who rejects Me and does not receive My sayings, has one who judges him; the word I spoke is what will judge him at the last day. John 12:47-48 NASB*

Jesus says, I will not be your judge; the Word of God will judge mankind. Therefore, it is so powerful to say, "it is written" to the fallen angels. Remember what I wrote at the beginning of the sub-title called, "The Power of the Word of God," when God spoke the heavens or creation into existence, and the breath or the Holy Spirit went forth to give those words life. The power of God's Word in that day will reward those who have been faithful and judge those who have not obeyed the Word. To some believers, they will barely escape the fire, but will have little eternal reward. To others, those who have surrendered to the Word of God, great rewards.

One day every believer will have to stand before God and recount their life here on earth. Can we imagine if God had us show up now before Him and give an account thus far on our life, we would tremble for what we have not done, and go to work and believe God immediately. Let me say it this way. When we open our Bibles and read the Word of God, we are reading the very thing that will judge us and reward us. If this is so concerning the fallen angels and sinners, do we think we will be exempt, NO! We have salvation in Christ, but we can suffer much loss of eternal rewards.

Second, in John 14:23 (NASB) it says,

> *Jesus answered and said to him, "If anyone loves Me, he will keep My word; and My Father will love him, and We will come to him and make Our abode with him.*

This is one of the few places in the Bible where the plural noun is mentioned about God. Jesus declares, the Father and the Son, will come to the believer through the Word of God. It is time the Church takes a different approach to the written Word. The Word of God is holy and we should treat it with reverence. Oh, the power of "IT IS WRITTEN."

CHAPTER NINE

RELEASING JUDGMENTS AND BLESSINGS

I would like for us to look at some scriptures found in the burning bush account. In Exodus 3:5

> *Then God said, "Do not come near; take your sandals off your feet [out of respect], because the place on which you are standing is holy ground." And God said, "Certainly I will be with you, and this shall be the sign to you that it is I who have sent you: when you have brought the people out of Egypt, you shall serve and worship God at this mountain." But I know that the king of Egypt will not let you go unless [he is forced] by a strong hand.*

I have noticed in the Church today that there is not much respect for the power of God. I see people talking, cell phones ringing, some sit and watch, and some go home. Whatever the case, I can tell these individuals have a low opinion of God's power. Moses' first reaction to the power of God was fear. I too remember when the power of God touched my life, it felt so good, but there was this fear of not knowing. I came to realize that the fear that felt so good was my first lesson. I had to learn to respect and honor the presence and power of God. I had been in the presence and power of a holy God.

When God visits a believer like He did me, He will be with you. God's presence and power will be with you. This is a sign to all mankind; If God is judging the powers of darkness, God is with that individual and His power follows that believer. Most believers do not understand the sign; they just form their own opinions. The power of God is to free mankind from the powers of darkness so they can serve God and worship God.

Let the godly ones exult in glory;
Let them sing for joy on their beds.
Let the high praises of God be in their throats,
And a two-edged sword in their hands,
To execute vengeance on the nations
And punishment on the peoples,
To bind their kings with chains
And their nobles with fetters of iron,
To execute on them the judgment written.
This is the honor for all His godly ones.
Praise the Lord! (Hallelujah!)
Psalm 149:5-9 AMP

CHAPTER NINE

The Hebrew word for "godly ones" (ḥā·sîḏ) means a special one dedicated and faithful. A person characterized by loyal love to God or the ones faithful to God as a group. It also refers to someone who is totally given to the Word of God or they tremble at God's Word.

We see an amazing series of statements in this psalm. We are to express exceeding joy in God's presence and we are to sing. The high praise the psalmist is talking about are words of honor, respect, reverence, and worship. The two-edged sword is more than two sharp sides of a blade; it is the Word of God. So we are to have the high praises of God in our mouths and the Word of God in our hands, which is the power of God. With these two principles, we can execute vengeance on the nations, which are the fallen angels. We can bring punishment on the fallen angels who influence the minds of men. We can bring punishment to people who do not repent. God's Word and His power is to bind in chains and fetters the fallen angels and to have them imprisoned. We are to have the leaders of nations imprisoned. These things happen when the believer goes forth in prayer and moves in power asking God for judgment according to God's written Word.

What I am saying is, we are to engage in combat with the Word of God and praises from our mouth, the fallen angels that rule the nations, but this is not our only battle. We are to take the Word of God and judge evil people who rule and not vote for them. We are to execute on the nations which is an honor or privilege, the judgments of God. What a great entitlement and honor the believer has been called too.

God has written judgments within His scriptures; we are not the ones who are to make the judgments. God has made the judgments, and we have the privilege of executing those judgments. God has called us to play our part in history. We are to study and find out what made America great, and vote that way. We are to study the Word of God and call for the judgment of the gods over the nation. However, there are many Christians who have never acted in like measure. They are so far away from these principles. What this shows is that most believers have not even understood what God expects from them.

When God sends down the fallen angels for judgment, we decree and declare the written judgments of God. The one engaged in combat is proclaiming God's Word, the laws of the creation, while others are speaking of the glories of God.

Stretch Out The Rod

What did Moses do when he reached Egypt, he stretched out the rod or demonstrated the power of God? We are to exercise the authority God has given the believer, like Moses, exercising the authority in his rod. Notice the rod was Moses'. We are to take the written Word of God and stretch it out against the gods, the fallen angels. When there is a situation when the authority of God is needed, like a sickness which could end one's life, we are to approach that situation in authority.

In scripture, one of the most effective ways to release the authority of God is by proclaiming in faith the written Word. When we are under the anointing of the Holy Spirit, remembering the Word must go with the Breath, the Holy Spirit, releasing it with our mouth, it has all the authority of Almighty God.

What most believers do today is pray to God. They demonstrate by asking God to take their authority out of their hands and do it Himself. This is actually backwards or opposite in thinking or according to God's Word. In Moses' account, God told Moses, you have the rod; you do it.

THE POWER OF PROCLAMATION

I am about to touch a subject that most believers never want to admit, sickness which can bring death is a spirit of infirmity.

I shall not die, but live,
And declare the works of the Lord.
The Lord has chastened me severely,
But He has not given me over to death.
Psalm 118:17-18 NKJV

What is the psalmist speaking about when he says, "the Lord has chastened me severely?" The definition is to chasten, admonish, and discipline. Let us just skim over these definitions and see what they tell us. To chasten is to humble or subdue someone. To admonish someone is to rebuke or reprimand. To discipline is to use punishment to correct disobedience. As one who has seen thousands healed and delivered, I understand that because of disobedience in one's life or in their generations, sickness is the curse. To rebuke as Jesus did, it means to hold someone accountable for wrongdoing. We must find out what the infirmity's legal rights are. This sickness to subdue is to bring death. Sickness that could bring death comes from the kingdom of darkness. So we pray to God for healing, declaring His Word regarding the matter. We also use the sword in action, seeking deliverance from the evil spirit of infirmity. We must cast out sickness that brings death.

We know from scripture that it is the will of the Lord to live a long and fruitful life and not die before our time. When someone is diagnosed with cancer, let's say first, it is a spirit and second, it is God's will to not give us over to an early death. Why is it so hard for mankind to believe, that sickness originates from the fallen angels, and at times, we must ask God to judge the fallen angel who holds the sickness?

No weapon formed against you shall prosper,
And every tongue which rises
against you in judgment
You shall condemn.
This is the heritage of the servants of the Lord,
And their righteousness is from Me,"
Says the Lord.
Isaiah 54:17 NKJV

The very first thing we should learn from this scripture is that the fallen angels are looking to form a weapon against us. What do these weapons look like? Jesus says, they are weapons that steal, kill, and destroy. We know things like poverty, sickness, vices, all keep us from thriving. How are weapons formed? The fallen angels use any instrument of war in hunting (temptation), fighting (false knowledge), and warfare (thoughts). The definition for a weapon is any instrument used in hunting, fighting or warfare. The Apostle Paul says the weapons of our warfare are not carnal, that means they are spiritual weapons. To fight in the spirit realm, we are to use spiritual weapons. The spiritual weapons we use are the promises of God proclaimed and acted on spiritually.

The word formed means to be planned or to be an object of planning. It is God's desire that the plans of the fallen angels fail. The fallen angels over someone's bloodline work hard to make their plan a success or reach a desired goal. How do some or all of the fallen angels' plans succeed? They have demons tempt for entry. Through false knowledge they lead us astray or into captivity. The warfare in our minds reveal strongholds against the Word of God.

Whether visible or invisible, every tongue which rises against the believer we shall proclaim guilty of wickedness or immorality. God has given believers the ability in Christ Jesus to proclaim the Word of God to the rulers and authorities in the heavenly realms their wickedness and immoral actions. This heritage or the believer's inheritance is the kingdom of God passed on to us through the works of Christ Jesus on the cross. We are to take those promises God has made to us in Christ Jesus and say, "IT IS WRITTEN."

> *The bolts of your gates will be iron and bronze,*
> *and your strength will equal your days.*
> *"There is no one like the God of Jeshurun,*
> *who rides across the heavens to help you*
> *and on the clouds in his majesty.*
> *The eternal God is your refuge,*
> *and underneath are the everlasting arms.*
> *He will drive out your enemies before you,*
> *saying, 'Destroy them!'*
> *Deuteronomy 33:25-27 NIV*

To ride is to sit and travel in a chariot while controlling motion. The definition states, to go to by land. God does not just sit enthroned or on a throne, He is all over the earth at the same time. In the New Testament use of the cloud theme, at the transfiguration God spoke out of a cloud to identify Jesus as "my Son, whom I have chosen" (Lk 9:35). Jesus, like God in the Old Testament, rides on a cloud (Acts 1:9). One of the most pervasive images of Christ's return is as one who rides his cloud chariot into battle (Mt 24:30; Mk 13:26; 14:62; Lk 21:27; Rev 1:7; cf. Dan 7:13).

God will destroy His enemies, but we must drive them out. We must use our authority in Christ to drive out all supernatural forces of evil. From the lowest of demons to

Satan himself, we are to take our authority or judicial control and exercise it over our territory. We must remember our enemies are not flesh and blood; they are the fallen angels in the second heaven.

How does this work? In deliverance, when God brings down the fallen angel, the minister needs to find out if its criminal or civil. If its criminal, it will be according to what we and our bloodline has done through iniquity, coupled together with the sins of society within the fallen angel's jurisdiction. If it is civil, usually it is according to what we've done personally, and what we have done to others. Put simply, which court are we in, civil or criminal? What is the jurisdiction of the fallen angel?

There is another reality we must look at. When a deliverance minister casts out demons personally or corporately, this is when the fallen angels are most active in people's thoughts and ideas, working to control their reasoning, causing negative judgments and finally rejecting what is taking place. Anyone with any spiritual understanding knows that deliverance cannot take place unless God is doing it.

Let us look at authority and power! Before anyone can rightly operate in a system of authority, we must know our parameters and restrictions. Authority, even in worldly systems, has parameters. Authority is the Greek word 'exousia', it refers to the right to use power, to take action, to issue commands, and to respond in obedience. This is key in using the power the right way; It takes understanding!

If I don't know or come into a revelatory understanding, I cannot command with power because I don't understand the sphere of authority I need to operate in.

To operate in authority, we must first understand whose authority we function under and to what level. Second, we must recognize and submit to authority over us. Third, we must understand the boundaries of our authority. Fourth, as we obey the first three listed, it is revealed to us that authority grows. Much like being promoted through your job. Fifth, we must learn the rules of engagement so we don't get in trouble. Much like the workplace, we can get in trouble if we go beyond our job description. I see many believers misusing God's authority. I see many believers misusing God's authority and falsely making claims of which they understand very little. Have you ever heard a believer say, "The devil has no power over me." Not realizing that the devil's authority and power over them is sin.

Since Satan is a fallen angel and has authority over evil in this Age, he must delegate his authority. The fallen angels by way of delegated authority, have power.

As we look again at Daniel 10, we find Daniel in a state of mourning and fasting some 21 days. Remember what Jesus said, this kind only comes out by prayer and fasting. Comes out of what? The Mind! God has moved Daniel in deep sorrow because of the desolation of the city of Jerusalem.

In those days I, Daniel, was mourning three full

CHAPTER NINE

*weeks. I ate no pleasant food, no meat or wine came
into my mouth, nor did I anoint myself at all, till
three whole weeks were fulfilled. Daniel 10:2-3*

As Daniel pursued an answer from God, Gabriel an arch-angel who was lower in rank than Michael visited him. Let us also remember before we get too far that Daniel 10-12 is a single continuous revelation of events. What is in play here? The future of Israel. It was Daniel's desire to know what God would do with Israel. Israel had been departing Babylon, and Daniel's heart was heavy over the rebuilding programs of the temple and wall. I believe this book series is the beginning of the rebuilding program of God. This book series may sound like new information, but it is God who is restoring what we lost through religion back to the Church.

The question is, are you that person like Daniel who set himself in prayer and warfare, one righteous man, through prayer and fasting, unleashes a cosmic battle that involves Chief Princes, Princes, and Kings of the highest angelic order. I am watching God deal with these fallen angelic rulers who influence the minds of mankind to reject Jesus Christ and to live for sin or to live for the fallen angels.

CHAPTER TEN

THE FALL OF THE DAY STAR

There is a day of tribulation coming upon the earth when the wicked and godless people are taken out and held in the torments of hell until the day of the great judgment. Until those days come, we are in a cosmic war with fallen angels and demonic spirits who seek to bring mankind under their judgment, which God judged and sentenced them to everlasting punishment.

The Bible refers to a day when the coming conflict in the second heaven takes place, but leaves little information on how or when this will happen. This end time battle between the angels of God and the fallen angels, it was not for past generations (to know), but for this present one and future generations to come.

As this battle heats up in this evil Age between the Church and the fallen angels, the fallen watchers will begin to shake, and great fear and trembling shall start to seize them as God's people move deeper into second heaven spiritual warfare and prayer in the courts of Heaven.

> *He who overcomes will inherit all this, and I will be his God and he will be my son. But the cowardly, the unbelieving, the vile, the murderers, the sexually immoral, those who practice magic arts, the idolaters and all liars—their place will be in the fiery lake of burning sulfur. This is the second death." Revelation 21:7-8 NIV*

When Isaiah described the fall of Lucifer, he spoke only about him, yet we know that one-third of the angels fell with him. Therefore, we know that when scripture mentions the devil, it indirectly speaks of the fallen angels. Isaiah calls Lucifer a morning star or a celestial body. There is another definition, and it refers to the crescent moon, which is seen on Islamic mosques and flags.

> *Whose minds the god of this age has blinded, who do not believe, lest the light of the gospel of the glory of Christ, who is the image of God, should shine on them. 2 Corinthians 4:4 NKJV*

Paul describes the devil as the god of this Age who has blinded the minds of mankind. When we combine Isaiah and Paul, we have a celestial body that rules over an evil Age. What the Bible is pointing us too, these celestial bodies are spheres of jurisdiction that will be present during the duration of this evil Age. Paul says, it is possible through the spread of the gospel and proper faith with works, the Church can bring down these evil fallen angels or celestial bodies as we enforce the rule of Christ.

When Isaiah says the fallen angels have weakened the nations, it speaks of defeating by acting against them. The Lexicon says that the fallen watchers have won a victory over the nations. The fallen angels began a military conflict against mankind and won. The fallen angels taught mankind to use the metals of the earth to make instruments of war to fill the earth with violence and bloodshed. From the lusts of the flesh came fornication and ungodliness. The fallen also taught mankind the covenants of the occult listed in Deuteronomy 18:10-12. Astrology is the study of the movements and relative positions of celestial bodies that have an influence on the affairs of mankind and the natural world. The key word, celestial, fallen angels in the second heaven taught mankind to worship them and how to tap the powers of a celestial realm or a fallen angel.

The First Book of Enoch contains details of a class of angels identified as the Watchers, who, against God's plans, came to earth to teach humankind all about weapons, spell potions, root cuttings, astrology, and astronomy, and alchemy. The Watchers had sex with human women, the result of which was the dark Naphilim. Enoch states that God punished them being ordering that they be bound in Tartarus. It also mentions this in the New Testament. However, most scholars and Bible teachers believe that they are in Tartarus now. In my encounters with the fallen watchers, I have come to experience that Tartarus is where they need to be sent.

When the fallen angels went into women, they produced sons called the Naphilim. Accord to who fathered them, that made them all dissimilar, different. Because of the evil in which the fallen angels and mankind did, they devoured each other. When the Naphilim started producing sons, they were called the Naphil, and Naphil produced the Eljo. Every crime known was committed, so it will be in the last days. The earth will be filled with bloodshed, injustice, and sin.

God has called the Church to cleanse the earth from all oppression as the gospel goes forth. To remove sin and all godlessness, the uncleanness that is done on the earth. We can only do this as the Church spreads the gospel with healing and deliverance power.

Through Jesus Christ, God has given the Church the power of understanding through wisdom. He has also empowered us through combat to reprimand the fallen angels. We do this through the wisdom and understanding of the Word or God, "It Is Written."

This book series has shown that the origin of evil spirits were when the Naphilim had sexual union with women. Since they were born on the earth, they shall live on the earth. Therefore, there cannot be any reason to call them demonic principalities. Since the hybrids were born from women and the Watchers, the Bible calls them evil or demonic spirits. These demonic spirits are the spirits of the giants and they will afflict, oppress, destroy, attack, war, kill, and cause trouble on the earth.

Demonic spirits need no food; they do not hunger or thirst; they are invisible, yet their function is to cause offenses against God and His Word. They war against mankind and seek bodily possession. The reason they can enter and possess a man is because they have proceeded from mankind. Because they are much like mankind, they can enter or possess mankind and seek control of man's mind and bodily functions. They are the disembodied spirits of the offspring of angels and humans.

My supernatural combat encounters with demonic spirits agree with what the Bible explains; upon the death of the giants, their spirits went out of their bodies and still have the ability to expose mankind to evil and heap upon their heads more of God's judgment until the day of Jesus' return. The Bible also states, the fallen angels or Watchers, and demon spirits will not be judged fully until Christ hands over the Kingdom of God to the Father after the Millennium.

We do know that at one time the fallen angels made their abode in heaven, but not all the mysteries of heaven had been explained or revealed to them. For example, they did not know when Jesus would appear on the earth. However, the mysteries they knew, they taught mankind and much evil was done on the earth.

There is a prison for the fallen angels or the host of heaven called Tartarus. The Bible Lexicon says it is not the abyss, but beyond the abyss. Like the deep or bottomless chasm, the regions of hell, better translated, the regions of judgment, there is no water, it too is a desert-like realm and indescribably horrible or torturous. The fallen will be sent there because they have transgressed the commandments of the Lord. We know they did not operate in their appointed times, but chose to abandon their seasons and abode to have sex with women.

Paul says in 1 Timothy 4:1; "The Spirit clearly says that in later times some will abandon the faith and follow deceiving spirits and things taught by demons." Paul tells us that the Holy Spirit precisely and clearly expressed to him that some will abandon the faith like the fallen angels did God, showing signs of continually distancing themselves from the truth found in Christ Jesus and giving up positions they may have held.

When I am in a second heaven deliverance with fallen angels, and the issues have been argued in the courts of heaven through the trial process, and I call for the eternal chains of darkness, the fallen angels scream. Tartarus is a fearful place and the visual performance or display of the fallen angels is of fear and pain. This place is the prison of the angels, and my biblical understanding is that they will be imprisoned there forever.

There is a place for mankind who follow the ways of sin. Hell is a gathering place of the dead, where the dead are gathered and whose end is the lake of fire.

*"Now there was a certain rich man who was habit-
ually dressed in expensive purple and fine linen,
and celebrated and lived joyously in splendor every
day. And a poor man named Lazarus, was laid at
his gate, covered with sores. He [eagerly] longed to
eat the crumbs which fell from the rich man's table.
Besides, even the dogs were coming and licking his
sores. Now it happened that the poor man died and
his spirit was carried away by the angels to Abraham's bosom (paradise); and the rich man also died
and was buried. In Hades (the realm of the dead),
being in torment, he looked up and saw Abraham
far away and Lazarus in his bosom (paradise).
And he cried out, 'Father Abraham, have mercy on
me, and send Lazarus so that he may dip the tip
of his finger in water and cool my tongue, because
I am in severe agony in this flame.' But Abraham
said, 'Son, remember that in your lifetime you
received your good things [all the comforts and
delights], and Lazarus likewise bad things [all the
discomforts and distresses]; but now he is comforted
here [in paradise], while you are in severe agony.
And besides all this, between us and you [people] a
great chasm has been fixed, so that those who want
to come over from here to you will not be able, and
none may cross over from there to us.' So the rich
man said, 'Then, father [Abraham], I beg you to
send Lazarus to my father's house— for I have five
brothers—in order that he may solemnly warn*

them and witness to them, so that they too will not come to this place of torment.' But Abraham said, 'They have [the Scriptures given by] Moses and the [writings of the] Prophets; let them listen to them.' He replied, 'No, father Abraham, but if someone from the dead goes to them, they will repent [they will change their old way of thinking and seek God and His righteousness].' And he said to him, 'If they do not listen to [the messages of] Moses and the Prophets, they will not be persuaded even if someone rises from the dead.'" Luke 16:19-31 AMP

Jesus reveals that there are places in the spirit world that are reserved for all evildoers, angels or mankind. Here their spirits shall be set apart in this great pain until the great day of judgment and punishment and torment of those who follow sins, curses, and retribution for their transgressions.

MORE ON PRINCIPALITIES AND POWERS

I designed this book series to advance our understanding of the second heaven's fallen angels. Spiritual warfare demands that we gain a working understanding of what these powers really are. My intent here is to make simple an obscure subject. What exactly do we "struggle" against? Who, or what, are these "principalities and powers"? How can we defeat them? How can the gospel spread unimpeded?

My expanded version of Ephesians 6:12 says this: For our wrestling match is not against flesh and blood [contending only with physical opponents], not against persons with bodies, but against cosmic powers or fallen angels within four levels of the celestial realm who rule in various areas and descending orders of authority. Against world dominators of this present evil age, and against spiritual forces of wickedness in the heavenlies who are orderly tiered.

Here is my explanation of my expanded version of the cosmic hierarchy: This pictures a very highly structured organization of levels and grades according to numbers within a hierarchy who are well organized as a kingdom of four different dimensions in the second heaven. These different kinds of fallen angels within each of the four dimensions have descending orders of authorities and different rulers and sub rulers according to grade and number responsible for different areas of authority in the second heaven which rule over the earth through the minds of mankind.

We know from Ephesians 1:21 and 6:12, and Colossians 1:6 and 2:15, that these are fallen spiritual beings that operate in satan's domain, opposing the redemptive purposes of God.

When we look closely and study what scholars write in both Old and New Testaments, with additional confirmation from Apocryphal texts, it reveals three categories of fallen angels: first, those angels who fell originally with Lucifer at the time of his rebellion and who are still active in the deception and affliction of people. Second, the "sons of God" or angelic beings of Genesis 6:2 who committed such abominable acts of immorality with the "daughters of men" (women), they were "bound with everlasting chains for judgment on the great Day" (Jude 6). Third, angelic beings who were given charge to watch and rule over certain groupings of mankind.

My finding in the supernatural and my studies of the Word of God revealed that one-third of the angels rebelled all at once. When all the angels in the heavens witnessed this rebellion and the fall, none have sinned since. Therefore one-third rebelled and sinned together, and their nature became corrupt. Because of this sinful, corrupt nature some, if not all, of the fallen angels had sexual relations with the human women. The Genesis six account groups all the fallen angels together by saying, the sons of God. Moses does not say, some sons of God, but the sons or all the fallen angels. God has sentenced the fallen angels to pits of darkness and everlasting chains for the day of judgment. Even though the fallen angels have been sentenced and judged, as long as this evil age continues, the sons of God await the inevitable. We can see this picture in Adam's sin; he spiritually died, but physical death awaited him. When this evil Age ends, then the judgment of God.

I have been in almost every level of spiritual warfare in the heavenly realms, and one thing I have learned, the Church can enforce that judgment now. Just as a man's life can be cut short for various reasons, so the Church does not have to wait for the evil Age to end.

According to the Septuagint text and recent scholarship, the clearer rendering here is "sons of God," angelic beings (cf. Job 38:7). Daniel 4:13 and 17 call these powers the "Watchers." Who are they? They are angels of a high order charged with divine authority and appointed to watch over certain segments of humanity.

When the Most High gave to the nations their
inheritance,
when he divided mankind,
he fixed the borders of the peoples
according to the number of the sons of God.
Deuteronomy 32:8 ESV

Scripture reveals and talks of the "council of Yahweh," heavenly beings who carry out the divine will (1 Kings 22:19; Ps. 89:6,7). We know that these angels, who call themselves fallen, lost positions of authority when they chose to leave God's Kingdom.

Paul brings light to the topic by depicting the powers as organized in a hierarchy of rulers/principalities (archai), authorities (exousia), powers (dunamis), and spiritual forces of evil (kosmokratoras). We can see the hierarchical system in Colossians 1:16 which lists them in order, thrones or dominions or principalities or powers.

The Apostle Paul tells us there were supernatural forces that "stood behind" human governments and all structures. We know from scripture and supernatural encounters that structures are businesses, organizations like the Masonic Lodge, churches, government parties, and so on. Paul understood from his travels and his interaction in the supernatural that cosmic beings from the second heaven interfered with his calling and mission.

Until the Judgment, God recognizes these forces and allows them to remain active. The world operates in the hostility of a transitional age when victory over darkness has been accomplished, but the redeemed struggle against evil. God allows the enemy to act as a tempter and tester. For the individual Christian who surrenders to God, the schemes of evil serve as the believer's growth in the faith.

These evil powers work through human governments, religions, and powerful people to keep individuals in bondage to legalism, social culture, and moral compromise. Their business is to pollute the minds and distort the wills of people, distracting them from redemption, holding them hostage to an Age of evil and lies.

SOCIETY OF DARKNESS

I have spoken several times about fallen angels, second heaven structures, the operations of the fallen angels, and how they order the demonization of an individual and mankind in general. Now I would like to turn our attention to something powerful and focus on the collective impact of demonized individuals in their society or subculture. We may be familiar with the classic phenomenon of extreme individual demonization, such as unusual strength, other voices, and exposure of private knowledge. But what are some factors of a society or subculture where the bulk of people are demonized?

CHAPTER TEN

I have seen areas in the United States where demonization has a major impact on its citizens. We call this the concept of collective captivity. It is the reality that demons working through individuals can control society to some extent and actively use the system to prevent the gospel from penetrating into individual lives. This reality brings oppressive laws and belief systems to subject mankind to evil. We see the true reality in red and blue states. Mostly, red states are open to capitalism and the spread of the gospel. Capitalism is where economic and political systems in which private owners control a country's trade and industry for profit, rather than by the state. Therefore, mankind lives in realms of freedom and makes the gospel available to all. However, blue states are more socialist in their laws. Blue states want state or government control so they should own and regulate individuals in all their affairs. Remember, we are talking about demonization as a collective society.

When the good news arrives, the second heaven fallen angelic strategies flow with the changing culture. The fallen angel's goal is to keep the demonized in dungeons of darkness, in a kind of collective captivity that discourages the individual from breaking free and into the Kingdom of light. Once the gospel penetrates the darkness, the fallen angels go to work through human demonization to stop the spread of the gospel. When the gospel is preached with demonstrations of the Holy Spirit, the fallen will use human systems, mainly money, and demonized people to block the spread of the gospel. The fallen angels will use demonized people not to give to a ministry, especially if it is a spiritual warfare and power ministry. They will convince individuals to stay clear of ministries who through spiritual warfare bring the kingdom of darkness out into the open.

I have also found that churches who resist the movement of the Holy Spirit, especially spiritual warfare, whether they believe in the baptism of the Holy Spirit and healing or not, are mostly demonized. Without direct confrontation, no one individual can be free. Jesus directly took on the devil in the wilderness, why should we deviate from that pattern?

Churches who have Sunday services like, twenty minutes of worship, announcements, and a message, all over in about one hour, are controlled by a fallen angel. The church leadership gives to the people a collective system organized by the fallen angel and his demonized people. I continue to preach that if worship doesn't bring an encounter; the message is not with power, and if there is no sign or wonder, get out!

Look at your city, the business in which you're employed, and your local church, do you see the collective impact of demonization through those groups? Are you aware of the culture that each organization has adopted? What your church allows determines how free the individual member is. The same is true with your city. What your city allows in its territory determines the demonization of each individual. For example, marijuana is becoming legal. The same is true of abortion and all sins that destroy godliness and family structure. These are signs that individuals who have voted in such a manner have cast their lot for a fallen angel to demonize their culture. There are some who say that they need not go to church to be a Christian, they do not see that they have undergone the process of deception and their minds have given way to a fallen angel and demonization. They may never admit it, but it does not cancel the reality.

What we allow into our cities affects society and the culture of that society. As stated above in different churches, business, and organizations, we see subcultures within people groups living together. Within a society or city, we have shared customs, laws, and organizations; these are subcultures that affect the overall culture in positive or negative ways. We have different customs or traditions within subcultures that over time, the fallen use to bring acceptance or tolerance. We have laws in our cities, states, and country that impact godliness and families in a positive or negative way. Even though we choose not to partake in laws that promote sinful activities and the destruction of families, we become tolerant and accepting. We allow organizations into our city that promote subcultures that do not have biblical standards or values, and so, give the fallen angels the right to demonize a city and each individual. We find these realities throughout the book of Acts.

PART TWO

~

INTERCESSION
LEAH HINES

CHAPTER ELEVEN

IT IS WRITTEN - LEAH

It's June 2019. My husband, Bruce, has spent the past 12 months writing this book series along with two other books. That's five books written and published in 12 months. I'm sure you agree with me when I say, "That is nothing but the Lord." because they are all packed full of wisdom, knowledge, combat experience, research, and details that go on and on! It's been thrilling to watch the Lord write through him. But it has come at a cost for our family.

Because of the Lord taking Bruce over for the past 12 months, our family has missed him. When he told me he was ready for a break, I was thankful. We took the time to plan our family vacation for the summer and fall. But before we began our summer adventure, my husband began to talk about how the Lord is speaking to him about the fourth book in this series.

Bruce told me he thought the series was over at three books. But being the intercessor I am, I knew in my knower that this series has multiple books. I can see it turning into at least six volumes. But we will all see and it seems it will be sooner than later.

When he started to say the title of his next book (which isn't this book it is book five) travailing intercession came over me! It overtook me! I kept hearing, "It is written." I knew at the moment that the Lord was calling me to partake in the writing process of this fourth book. So here I am writing to you about something so Holy, so God encountering, so humbling, something I am in love with; travailing intercession.

"The Holman Bible dictionary defines intercession as the act of intervening or mediating between differing parties, particularly the act of praying to God on behalf of another person."

"Logos 8 Bible software word study breaks down intercession as–to sigh; groan; lament; to vocally indicate pain, discomfort, or displeasure–to groan within oneself (complain)."

The Holy Spirit is formally filing a complaint about evil, sin, and injustice to God. Some know or call it travail.

Let's read Romans 8:26 where we find that the Holy Spirit is the one who prays through us when we travail.

> *In the same way the Spirit [comes to us and] helps us in our weakness. We do not know what prayer to offer or how to offer it as we should, but the Spirit Himself [knows our need and at the right time] intercedes on our behalf with sighs and groanings too deep for words.*
> *Romans 8:26 Amplified Bible (AMP)*

Did you read over the words sighs and groanings? Isn't it interesting how we can do that? Read right over key-words! I wonder how much of that is the Spirit hiding things for us to stimulate our natural desire to seek things out. Travailing intercession is a hidden secret, only for the seeker of the deep things of God!

Romans 8:26 shows us that the Holy Spirit is the one who prays through us when we travail. He intercedes on our behalf with sighs (some versions say unspeakable yearnings) and groanings. Some Bible teachers teach this passage as a passage about speaking in tongues. But a tongue is a prayer language, something with words. There are no words in travail, but sounds and emotions.

These two words, sigh, and groaning, are too important to help us understand what travail is for us not to look at how Logos 8 breaks them down.

In the Hebrew, the word groan means to sigh, scream,

growl, roar and moan—the Greek adds to groan together. The intercessor should always pay extra attention to passages that use these words.

I will continue to unfold more scriptures and definitions of what it is to travail along with my intimate experiences. Pay attention to when I give more word definitions about this different kind of prayer. Notice how the word definitions use the same words, intertwining the words together.

My Orders

In 2012, I was at our usual Thursday night prayer meeting in Waco Texas. My husband, Bruce, was standing at the microphone reading through Jeremiah 9. I'm lying prostrate with my face to the ground as he reads. When He got to verse 20, an overwhelming feeling of Power and Authority consumed my entire being. It took me over so intensely that I could no longer hear what my husband was reading. When he finished, the room went silent. When the feeling started to lift, I picked up my head to say, "Read it again!" This time, the Holy Spirit was flowing through me causing travailing sounds to push out of my mouth. When Bruce got to verse 20, the Lord audibly spoke to me saying, "This is what I created you to do." Making Jeremiah 9:20 my life scripture.

Now, you women, hear the word of the Lord;
open your ears to the words of his mouth.
Teach your daughters how to wail;
teach one another a lament. Jeremiah 9:20 (NIV)

The Lord of hosts gave these women a command. After what the Lord spoke to me, I receive it as a command from my Commander and Chief for my life. I would like to submit to you that this is a command for the travailing intercessor both male and female.

The Lord is commanding us to teach travailing intercession. Have you ever had such a heavy burden to pray for someone or something that it sent you into uncontrollable tears? Well, beloved, you have had the honorable experience of the Lord praying through you. We call this kind of prayer, travailing intercession.

Here are some word definitions from Logos 8 for the word wail from Jeremiah 9:20 - to howl, lament, TO YELL, TO WAIL; to cry out, make a noise, uproar; roar; give a sound; restless; groan.

For all you visual learners like me, I've added this word graph from Logos 8. It breaks down the word "roar" from the word definition of wail. I'm connecting the word roar with the word wail because this is how travail happens in me. Every word in the definition above describes what happens when I go through the process of travail. This visual brings me so much joy and excitement because it confirms travail.

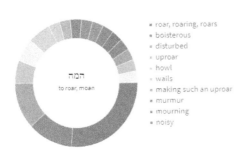

Remember how I said that travail is about sounds and emotions? Do you see here in this word graph sounds and emotions? When the Holy Spirit prays through us, we feel what He feels. I am sure it's a minute portion of His feelings, but they are there.

I lost my mom in March this year. That grief that I felt about the loss of my mom was very familiar to me. The Holy Spirit's grief that I feel about sin in the world is the same as I felt for months after I lost my mom. The only difference is, when it's the Holy Spirit's grief, it's momentary. It comes quickly, and it leaves quickly. That is why we wail, cry out, and weep. We are feeling emotional pain; we feel remorse, sorrow to where we want to repent. Yes, we understand that we didn't do the sin, but we are sorry because we feel how it hurts the Lord's heart. It is noisy! The pain is real but temporary.

Years ago, my mom went through a time where she didn't want to leave the house. She told me every time she would go out, she would always feel other people's pain. Interesting enough, I taught my Mother how to release the pain. I told her she was experiencing intercession for the people she was encountering. She didn't need to keep the pain. She just needed to ask the Holy Spirit to teach her to let Him push out their pain through her. It works as a washing. The Lord uses intercessors to take on the pain that is overwhelming others. You know it as a burden. One key every intercessor must know is how to release. You never need to hold on to others' pain. When the rivers of living water (I'll teach more about these rivers in my next chapter) push through you, they are washing away the pain of others. That is standing in the gap.

> *And I sought a man among them who should build up the wall and stand in the gap before Me for the land, that I should not destroy it, but I found none. Therefore have I poured out My indignation upon them; I have consumed them with the fire of My wrath; their own way have I repaid [by bringing it] upon their own heads, says the Lord God. Ezekiel 22:30-31 Amplified Bible, Classic Edition (AMPC)*

I remember the time when I was praying and asking the Lord about the effectiveness of my prayer life. He responded saying "You do not understand what your prayers prevent." Isn't that true?

When the intercessor stands in the gap, we stand between the Father and the Land (and/or people) crying out for His mercy. He doesn't want to pour out his indignation, the fire of His wrath or repay us our own ways. He would much rather have an intercessor to stand in the gap and PRAY!

I didn't think about this until now, but I often pray that Jesus will stand between an individual and all the forces of darkness. In this prayer, I'm asking for an intercessor. For the Holy Spirit to stand between. Isn't He the one who is on the earth praying through us? I think I'll change my prayer now to "Holy Spirit, I pray that YOU will stand between all the forces of darkness and _____ (fill in the blank)."

Another emotion that the travailing intercessor will feel is anger! The Lord is angry over sin. When we feel His anger, it comes out as a groan or a roar. The anger intermixes with the Lords Power and Authority. This is when travail will push back the darkness. My husband can command a demon to leave with his words, where my authority comes from travail. For me, I always travail or ROAR out the demons, even the fallen. For demons, I've learned to turn on the roar, but for the fallen I have to have the Holy Spirit do that himself. Meaning, I can't turn that level of travailing warfare on. I don't have a switch to turn on warfare in the 2nd Heaven. I don't know if that will change, but I know that the fallen realm is the Lord's. Therefore, I expect He will always hold that switch.

OUR FIRST DATE

My first experience of this different prayer was on my first date with my now AMAZING husband! On our first date, we were still in the testing phase!

Years before we met, Bruce had a prophetic word that he would marry an intercessor who would complement him in the spirit realm and who could pray at the same level of the deliverance and healing realm that he would operate in. My first test was on our first date. He took me to a home fellowship where he had been hanging out with Christians 20 to 30 years old in the Lord.

We are eating dinner, when suddenly, this lady makes this super strange clicking noise. It was the strangest thing I'd experienced ever! I felt this turning in my stomach. I did not like the sounds coming out of her. I realize now, my un-renewed flesh was crying out. In her maturity, she excuses herself from the dinner table and goes into the master bedroom. I did not understand the clicking noise was intercession, until months later. She knew she should not stop the Lord from travailing through her and that she should not put the dinner guests through the experience. I don't remember ever talking with Bruce about it on that day, but the memory and feelings from the whole experience are still with me today. I'm thankful I went through that because I know what others feel when they see me travailing. The devil lies to make us think what is happening isn't from the Lord.

After we ate dinner, we all moved into the living room to pray. For the first time, I felt what they felt in Acts when they prayed in one accord. We all sat in seats that put us in a circle. Everyone started out with praying in tongues, their heavenly language. It wasn't long until I felt a STRONG flowing of the Lord's presence. This flow started at one part of the circle and made its way around. I could feel the Holy Spirit moving through the circle. The entire circle, not just when He came to me. I felt His flow; He felt like waves washing over us.

Have you ever seen the wave at a sporting event? At first, you're chatting with your friends around you. Suddenly, you notice the wave has started. Then you watch it, with the joy of it coming to you. Seeing when to stand, you watch the crowd to know the timing. Waiting, watching, and expecting until it arrives at your section. And then BAM, you stand while throwing your hands into the air and sit back down to expect again.

That is exactly what was happening in this circle of prayer warriors, mature Christians! The only difference was that I could also feel the wave coming and continuing to flow through the rest of the circle. When the wave hit each person, we would pray more intensely. It was the most wonderful thing I had the pleasure of experiencing, so far in my life! I didn't want to leave.

Later in the evening after a Bible study, they all started prophesying over everyone. When it was my turn some ladies were praying over me. They were saying "bars of intercession" as they were laying their hands on my stomach. I did not understand what bars of intercession meant. But boy would I know soon enough. What a great first date!

BARS OF INTERCESSION

Therefore My heart moans and sighs for Moab like flutes, and My heart moans and sighs like flutes for the men of Kir-heres (Kir-hareseth); therefore [the remnant of] the abundant riches they gained has perished. Jeremiah 48:36 Amplified Bible, Classic Edition (AMPC)

When I am travailing, I flow from weeping to roaring to

sounding like a flute to groaning and then moaning. The Lord plays me like a wind instrument.

"Wikipedia gives the definition of an orchestra as a group of instrumentalists, especially one combining string, woodwind, brass, and percussion sections. Orchestras are usually led by a conductor who directs the performance with movements of the hands and arms, often made easier for the musicians to see by the use of a conductor's baton. The conductor unifies the orchestra, sets the tempo and shapes the sound of the ensemble."

When we pray in one accord, it is like an orchestra. It is a group of people flowing together being directed by the Holy Spirit. We are the instruments and He is the breath blowing through us while conducting us at the same time. The more musicians you have in an orchestra the more beautiful it sounds. It's the same for travail, the more intercessors the more beautiful it is to the Lord.

Just like each instrument makes its own unique sound, each intercessor will make a different sound. Some will only weep, while others will make sounds of a flute. The Lord will play others in just one or two different ways. Don't get hung up on that. It's up to the Lord to play us how he has designed us. Trust in the Lord and let his joy consume you in whatever way He desires!

CHAPTER TWELVE

I DIDN'T CHOOSE THIS

A few months after our first date in 2003, I was visiting with my aunt at her home in Plano, Texas. We were sitting around the living room talking about the Lord, like we always do. Soon, it was time for me to go pick up my brothers who would come hang out at my Aunts. As I was leaving, I could feel a sweet presence of the Lord that lingered after our talk.

My husband (boyfriend during this time) had taught me a special principle. The Holy Spirit is a gentleman. He will visit you, but His presence will lift a little to be sure you still want him to stay. When He lifts, keep engaging Him so He feels welcome.

Knowing this, I pushed into his presence by worshiping him in my car. When I did, the presence increased. It was so strong on me that when I stopped for gasoline; I kept singing. The presence took me over by my spirit. All my spirit wanted to sing was "Holy." When I got out of the car to pump my gas, I didn't care who could hear me, all I wanted to do was worship and keep singing, Holy! I did, I kept singing Holy as I pumped my gas. I got back in the car and continued to sing "Holy, Holy, Holy" repeatedly. I could feel my spirit desiring more and more of the Holy Spirit. I had this overpowering instinct to encounter more of the Godhead!

When I made it to George Bush, Highway 161, I started to say something that I didn't understand. Looking back today, I know; it was my spirit crying out. It was saying, "I want to know the fear of the Lord." I must have said it 10 times. Each time I said it, I could feel a desire growing from my belly. But it went in deeper, inside of me; to a deep place in my belly that overtook my being. Then suddenly this bubbling, gurgling noise came up out of me. I always think of that scripture about rivers of living water flowing from the innermost being. It literally felt like bubbles were coming out of me. Like when a water well first springs forth water, the water will bubble up before it flows out. It was the most amazing feeling. It felt like pure ecstasy, a complete joy. I prayed this way until I pulled into my brother's driveway. As soon as I parked the car, it stopped. I did not understand what just happened. But I knew it was the Lord.

CHAPTER TWELVE

He who believes in Me [who adheres to, trusts in, and relies on Me], as the Scripture has said, 'From his innermost being will flow continually rivers of living water. John 7:38 Amplified Bible (AMP)

I love this scripture because it expresses exactly what happens when the Holy Spirit prays through me with travail. When travail flows out of me, it's a continual flow from my belly. It can come on powerfully like a tidal wave, all at once and suddenly it's over. The intensity of the tidal wave will take me to the ground, on my knees. I cannot stand up. Other times, it's soft and steady the entire time. But then it can also be like a rain shower. A drizzle turns into a downpour then goes back to a drizzle. This can happen repeatedly or continually. I don't pick when I travail. It's on an as-needed basis.

Imagine you're in a room full of 200 people, and suddenly you groan and weep loudly! I'm remembering a time my husband and I were at a deliverance meeting. He started to minister to a woman who had an African Voodoo demon. The demon came up, I went down! Down to the ground, groaning with utterances not understood. All eyes were on me! But I could not control what the Lord was doing. Thankfully, everyone let it happen, and the demon left the woman. This is part of the humiliation I mentioned in the last chapter. It truly is humiliating, but oh so worth the price. If I didn't let the Lord war through me, Jesus wouldn't have delivered the woman that day. The Lord has a plan and a strategy for everything. It's our choice to submit to what He is doing, not the other way around.

I want to talk about the feast of Tabernacles, which is where Jesus was when he was teaching in John 7. But first we need to dig into the words flow and continual, because they are both too important to pass them over. Travailing intercession comes from the deep things of God. That puts us in the deep end where you dig in to find the treasures that God has hidden away for us! Isn't that exciting? By now (this far into this book) you already know that we do this through word study, looking at the root of words in the Greek, Hebrew, and some Aramaic.

> *And when he came to the den and to Daniel,*
> *he cried out in a voice of anguish. The king*
> *said to Daniel, O Daniel, servant of the living*
> *God, is your God, Whom you serve continually,*
> *able to deliver you from the lions? Daniel 6:20*
> *Amplified Bible, Classic Edition (AMPC)*

The Bible lexicon says continually means without interruption, faithfully, continually. Without cessation, although there may be intervals between its presence; that which regularly recurs throughout a period. Daniel served the Lord in this way. His relationship was constant. In this same way, intercession is constant. The Lord, is always with the intercessor and the intercessor is constantly being used by the Lord giving him full access to their spirit. For those who know me, know travail comes on me anytime. As I've matured, I've learned how to hold it and release it when it's appropriate. But not in the beginning. I asked the Lord to teach me how to turn on and off the switch He uses! I am grateful that He did. But I still recognize it in young intercessors. If they let me, I like to help them learn how to control the flow.

I am grateful for the time I received the "whoa" because saying "whoa" is so much more receivable than roaring like a lion in a group of strangers. Let me try to explain. Bruce and I went to a meeting where Rolland and Heidi Baker where ministering. There were definitely over 1,000 people at this meeting. At one of the breaks, Rolland was in the entrance to the meeting room laying hands on people and getting them slain in the spirit. There had to be at least 200 people in this area. As he is laying hands on these people, they are all laughing and saying "whoa". But, when he lays his hands on me, I slam to the ground and start weeping, deeply and crying loudly with tears pouring down my face. I'm not sad; I feel tremendous joy in my spirit. I'm happy because I feel the Lords heart. But, others think I'm in distress or I'm manifesting demons. So naturally they come over to pray for me. Which then my husband explains that it's travailing intercession and I'm fine. After a few minutes, my tears turn into a mighty roar. Yes, like a lion! I'm roaring in this room of around 200 people who are rolling on the ground laughing their guts out. But, people keep coming over to me to pray, assuming I must be having a hard time.

After the meetings, I'm traveling home asking Jesus for the "whoa". I wanted to have some sound that was more receivable to others. People don't question that for some reason. If you just randomly say "whoa" in the middle of a conversation, nobody will question it. They may giggle a little, but they don't ask you if you need prayer or try to lay hands on you. Plus, in the circles that I run in, they understand the "whoa."

Well, Bruce and I went on an overnight trip to Bethel in Redding California. Unknown to me, some would say the home of the "whoa". But, long story short, I got the "whoa" while I was there. I don't know when it happened, but since that trip I now make the sound "whoa" when I'm in public situations where roaring like a lion is inappropriate. Okay, yes that is most public situations.

Now let's move on to the word flow. Travail is a continual flow of the Power and Authority of the Spirit with intervals of periods of intensity that flow like the rain that creates rivers. To flow means to flow as a liquid, to pour, to spill out, to go towards something. Bible commentators who reference John 7:38 with Ezekiel 47:8-9 say the rivers will go into a region. They will spill out from the region into the ocean. Travailing intercession is something that travails for the entire world. The travailing waters will reach the regions, the sea and cause everything to have life. Verse 9 prophetically says every living creature that gathers in places of travail, where ever the river goes, will live. Bringing the life that makes everything fresh.

Then he said to me, these waters pour out toward the eastern region and go down into the Arabah (the Jordan Valley) and on into the Dead Sea.

*And when they shall enter into the sea [the sea
of putrid waters], the waters shall be healed and
made fresh. And wherever the double river shall go,
every living creature which swarms shall live. And
there shall be a very great number of fish, because
these waters go there that [the waters of the sea]
may be healed and made fresh; and everything
shall live wherever the river goes. Ezekiel 47:8-
9 Amplified Bible, Classic Edition (AMPC)*

For the sake of having multiple scriptures to prove this
statement of how the Lord flows through the Intercessor
Rivers of living water that bring life here is Joel 3:18. Remember how I was talking about the first time I travailed?
Well, after I parked the car in my brother's driveway, I lead
my brother to the Lord. That was part of what the Holy
Spirit was praying for. I also believe that is proof of the life
that these rivers of living water will bring as we allow the
Holy Spirit to travail.

*And in that day, the mountains shall drip with
fresh juice [of the grape] and the hills shall flow
with milk; and all the brooks and riverbeds of
Judah shall flow with water, and a fountain
shall come forth from the house of the Lord
and shall water the Valley of Shittim. Joel 3:18
Amplified Bible, Classic Edition (AMPC)*

See how the river comes from the Lord? This kind of
prayer is only done by the Lord. It's meant to bring the will
of the Father to the earth. We hear it being said "Bringing

Heaven to Earth."

Bringing heaven to earth is about bringing the Father's will to earth. To the individual, to a family, a region, a church building, to where ever the Lord wants it to be.

And He Who searches the hearts of men knows what is in the mind of the [Holy] Spirit [what His intent is], because the Spirit intercedes and pleads [before God] in behalf of the saints according to and in harmony with God's will. Romans 8:27 Amplified Bible, Classic Edition (AMPC)

Remember, Romans 8:26 talks about how the Holy Spirit will pray through us when we don't know how to pray? Well, I love verse 27 because it shares with us an insight into the relationship of the Holy Spirit and the Father. The Holy Spirit is already in harmony with the Father's will. He already agrees with everything the Father wants. When He is praying through us, it automatically takes us before the Father, in our spirits. That rushing river of living water is gushing out the highest, most perfect will of the Father. There is only one correct way to pray. It's to praying the will of the Father. We don't ask or hope for our way to work out. We should pray to seek His will and then pray accordingly. Hoping the Lord does it our way is not the best way. If we want God's best, we will seek Him until we know His way, His will and then our prayers will follow suit.

But we can't read over the beginning of verse 27 because

this gives us an insight into the Holy Spirit's relationship with us. He searches our hearts. He wants to know what we need prayer for. I love the entire Psalm 139. Here is the first verse, but I hope you read the full chapter.

> *O Lord, you have searched me [thoroughly] and have known me. Psalm 139 Amplified Bible, Classic Edition (AMPC)*

He will search us and does search us. His whole intent is to know how to pray for us. Isn't that attribute of God intriguing? What a loving God we serve, that He would search out our needs! I get it, yes He already knows us through and through. He went ahead of us and goes behind us, while at the same time he is searching us. Knowing us with the intent of revealing us to heal us, to prepare us, to make us as much like Christ as we will allow. The number one priority of the Father's will is to bring Glory to Himself and to His son, Jesus Christ. In other words, He wants to reveal us so He can be revealed.

Because it's too powerful, too important for our relationship with the Godhead, I have to invite you to take your time and pray this bold prayer at the end.

> *God, I invite your searching gaze into my heart.*
> *Examine me through and through;*
> *find out everything that may be hidden within me.*
> *Put me to the test and sift through all my anxious cares.*
> *See if there is any path of pain I'm walking on,*

and lead me back to your glorious, everlasting
ways—
the path that brings me back to you. Psalm
139:23-24 The Passion Translation (TPT)

There is a difference between praying in different tongues and travail. When we pray in tongues, we are bringing glory to the Father by telling of the mighty works of God (Act 2:11) and we are building up our own spirits (Jude 20:20). We are speaking mysteries (1 Cor 14) according to the will of God. We edify and improve ourselves. But when we travail, we are birthing the Father's will, from Heaven into the earth.

My little children, for whom I am again suffering
birth pangs until Christ is completely and perma-
nently formed (molded) within you Galatians
4:19 Amplified Bible, Classic Edition (AMPC)

This kind of prayer impacts entire families, bloodlines, churches, regions, cities, nations and even the world. One of my favorite things to say about God is that He is eternal, He thinks eternally; He speaks eternally, and He acts eternally. Travail is a sound heard coming out of Zion (Jeremiah 9:19) creating a response from eternity into the earth.

That was an overview of the differences. I'd need to write my own series of books (hint, hint) to cover all the differences. But I hope you get the idea. They are important and valuable on their own. They are necessary for the growth of the individual and the growth of the church.

One extraordinary thing about the kingdom of God is that it is never-ending. We can always learn more!

Okay, now to discuss when Jesus was speaking at the Festival of Tabernacles in John 7. Both Jews and Gentiles were welcome at this festival. The festival is to teach all the people how to fear the Lord! Jesus is talking to us about more than the outpouring of the Holy Spirit.

This is what the Faithlife Study Bible says according to my Logos 8 Bible software.

"John 7:37 the last day of the feast Jewish tradition prescribes additional rituals for the final day of the festival—the culmination of their weeklong prayers for deliverance (according to the Babylonian Talmud Sukkah 53a).

If anyone is thirsty A subtle appeal to imagery of messianic deliverance associated with the Feast of Tabernacles. Jesus makes the point that He is the source of life—a claim that only God could make. This would have provoked His opponents, but it brought comfort to His followers.

A ritual of bringing water from the pool of Siloam and pouring it at the base of the altar was part of the daily festival celebration. This ritual memorialized the miracle of water from the rock in the wilderness (Num 20:2–13) and became symbolic of hope for messianic deliverance (Isa 12:3). The Festival of Tabernacles was associated with God providing rain (Zech 14:16–18), and Zech 14 was to be read on the first day of the feast (according to the rabbinic text Babylonian Talmud Megillah 31a). The seventh day of the festival, the last official day (Lev 23:34, 41–42), had a special water-pouring ritual and lights ceremony (according to the rabbinic text Mishnah Sukkah 4.9–10; 5.2–4). The festival came to be a celebration of God's future restoration of Israel and the extension of salvation to the nations. Jesus' invitation draws on those expectations of future ideal reality under the rule of the Messiah. (r2)"

It thrilled me to read how this ritual of pouring the water out at the altar expressed some results of travail; this rushing river of spiritual water that flows out of us. This ritual shows what we pray for, even when we don't know exactly what we are praying. The travailing intercessor will stand in the gap for miracles, deliverance, salvation, and the return of Christ.

On pg. 21 In "Christ's Last Order; Go Into All the World. By Derek Prince" "Christ's final orders to the body of Christ are to go into all the world.

- In Matthew 28- "all the nations," and "to the end of the age."

- In Mark 16- "all the world," and "every creature."

- In Acts 1- "to the end of the earth."

Do you see how in Jesus Christ's last words how He covers all time and all things in the physical realm? He has left nothing uncovered. These are the places travailing intercession cover; all time, all future, all past, all nations, all creatures, every geographical area in the world. An intercessor will be in their prayer closet crying out in these places through their spirit with the Holy Spirit. Why? Because travail is like the military's point man, it goes out FIRST!

CHAPTER THIRTEEN

JESUS TRAVAILED - MIRACLES AND INTERCESSION

D id you know that Jesus travailed before He raised Lazarus from the dead and before he delivered the man from the deaf and dumb spirit?

John 11:38-44–cried out means to scream (Hebrew Def. of intercession); to shout or cry out, with the implication of the unpleasant nature.

Let's look at the shortest scripture in many of the versions of the Bible.

Jesus wept. John 11:35 Amplified Bible (AMP)

The sense of the word "wept" is to cry (tears) – to shed

tears because of sadness, rage, or pain.

Read over this word study graph of the word "wept" from the Logos 8 Bible software Septuagint Translation.

נטף
to drip, secrete; to drivel, foam at the mouth, prophesy ecstatically

נתך
to gush forth; to pour out; to bring to the melting point

δακρύω
weep; shed tears

רעם
to be humbled, humiliated, brought low; to oppress, bring low, irritate

The Jews at the time thought Jesus was crying because he was mourning for the death of his friend. I beg to differ. Come on! If you read the entire story, Jesus already knew what would happen. He told the messenger what would happen. As you read the story, it gives the impression that the disciples overheard the plan. I expect the messenger took the news or the plan of the Father back to the sisters, Mary, and Martha. But they didn't comprehend what Jesus was saying.

Why would He be grieving for losing his friend when he understood what was getting ready to happen? He knew he would raise Lazarus from the dead. He knew the Father would use the situation to honor the Father and bring Glory to the son of God. (John 11:4) There is no way He was crying because of His grief for losing His friend.

CHAPTER THIRTEEN

He was weeping continually as he went because He knew that travailing intercession was the precursor to miracles. He wept because He could feel the grief of the Holy Spirit over ALL sin, ALL death. He was preparing the atmosphere for what was getting ready to happen.

There is a progression of intercession as you see Jesus move in the different waves of travail. This chapter is the intercessors' dream to teach. Yes, this is a testimony of the miraculous. But I see past that to the precursor, to the WAR that must happen to bring down Heaven to earth!

Watch the progression of travailing intercession. Go two verses up to John 11:33

When Jesus saw her sobbing, and the Jews who came with her [also] sobbing, He was deeply moved in spirit and troubled. [He chafed in spirit and sighed and was disturbed.] John 11:33 Amplified Bible, Classic Edition (AMPC)

Jesus begins by being deeply moved in His spirit and troubled. In the deep place in our spirit is where travail begins; in the place where we are one with the Holy Spirit, where He prays through us. You see where the Holy Spirit is praying through Jesus. He is feeling the anger (troubled in His spirit) because of sin and death in the world.

When the travailing intercessor feels this same anger, it is mixed with Power and Authority to drive out evil. It's a wave of righteous anger! This is when I roar! At first, I am

179

troubled (moved) by the unrighteousness and then I feel the anger because of the sin and then I feel the expression of the Holy Spirit through the troubling in my spirit.

The Septuagint translation says a lot about this one word, troubled. It says to make a noise, to be tumultuous, turbulent, to roar, to moan. It gives another sense of the word troubled as, to move, to sway backward and forwards.

In verse 34 is where they begin to walk; Jesus asks where they laid him. They say, Lord, come and see. In verse 35 is where Jesus wept. He is walking and weeping.

In verse 36, it says how the Jews thought he loved him tenderly. But that wasn't why He was weeping. Remember, I said He wept by the Holy Spirit because of His grief over ALL sin, ALL death.

Now in verse 38 they are approaching the tomb; walking up to the tomb. Jesus moves from weeping into sighing and deeply disquieted.

Now Jesus, again sighing repeatedly and deeply disquieted, approached the tomb. John 11:38 Amplified Bible, Classic Edition (AMPC)

Can you see how Jesus wept as they went? Look at the study graph for the word wept.

CHAPTER THIRTEEN

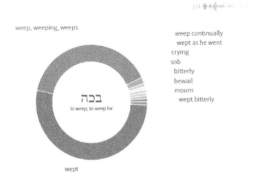

Doesn't it say "as he went"? You can see from the place, when they say come and see, that Jesus publicly travailed, with weeping, moaning, roaring, groaning and crying out from the debts of his belly the entire time He walked to Lazarus' grave. Did you read over the words again and repeatedly? It wasn't a little tear that came out of his eye and rolled down his face. It was a tumultuous, loud, noisy process that happened during the walk from when he asked where they laid him to when they arrived at his grave.

JESUS TRAVAILS BEFORE HE DELIVERS

Mark 7:31-36–Probably the deaf person's family or friends brought him to Jesus, acting as an intercessor. This means that their faith is part of the equation. The family or friends pleaded with Jesus to put His hands on him, the laying on of hands.

Jesus feels intercession, so Jesus takes the deaf man to a place that He could groan or travail because it was mostly a Gentile crowd. In intercession, Jesus does exactly what the Father wants, fingers in the ears and then spitting saliva

Jesus touches the man's tongue. Jesus gets the intercessory breakthrough and then declares "Be Opened."

The crowd went out and proclaimed the works of Jesus. There is something miraculous about testifying of the glories of God. We don't testify about a person or a church, but a place where Jesus can move.

Here is what my husband, Bruce Hines, says about this scripture in Volume 5: "Exploring Secrets of the Heavenly Realms: How fallen angels block healing. By Bruce Hines."

"Now let us look at the same Greek word "bond" in Mark 7:31-37

> *Again, departing from the region of Tyre and Sidon, He came through the midst of the region of Decapolis to the Sea of Galilee. Then they brought to Him one who was deaf and had an impediment in his speech, and they begged Him to put His hand on him. And He took him aside from the multitude, and put His fingers in his ears, and He spat and touched his tongue. Then, looking up to heaven, He sighed, and said to him, "Ephphatha," that is, "Be opened."*

> *Immediately his ears were opened, and the [l] impediment of his tongue was loosed, and he spoke plainly. Then He commanded them that they should tell no one; but the more He commanded them, the more widely they proclaimed*

*it. And they were astonished beyond measure,
saying, "He has done all things well. He makes
both the deaf to hear and the mute to speak."*

Jesus directed His vision upward, or the extended meaning is to discern or perceive. Jesus discerned that a principality or fallen angel held the legal right in the second heav-
en and the course of action here was a deep sigh. The word
"sigh" here means to groan. There are many definitions to
groans in the Hebrew-Greek. Just a few, to mutter, growl,
roar, moan, lament, groan together or travail together with
the Holy Spirit. Today, we call this travailing intercession.

The man could not hear or speak, so travailing intercession appealed to the heavenly court on behalf of the man.
Jesus was on the earth, the fallen angel was in the second
heaven, and Jesus appealed to God's court in the highest
of heavens. When Jesus went into sighing, the fallen angel had to come down and Jesus pleaded this man's case
in the courtroom of God. This is a textbook case for both
the intercessor and deliverance minister. Many times I've
been in a deliverance session where my wife who moves in
travailing intercession will begin groaning, sighing, that is
travail. The Holy Spirit will come upon her when we do
not know what to pray or which direction the deliverance
session should go. It is the Holy Spirit who offers travailing
prayer and how to offer it through sounds and groaning
too deep for words or tongues. The Holy Spirit helps us in
our weakness and He Himself pleads the case."

I want to say how thankful I am for my husband! He

has stood by me in my walk through this beautiful gift of travailing intercession. When we are in public and I can't control how the Holy Spirit is praying through me my husband will stand right next to me, guarding me. See, people don't understand travail. They think I am hurting, in pain. I know their intentions are good. I realize they want to help me by laying their hands on me and praying. Thankfully, my husband will gently tell them I am fine and how I am travailing with the Holy Spirit.

One of my favorite word definitions for "sigh" is "to sound a battle cry." There are noises that come out of me that I know get the attention of angles. It's as certain sound they are drawn to and alerted to go to war. I like to plug in this word definition when Jesus sighed in Mark 7:34.

> *Then, looking up to heaven, He sounded a battle cry, and said to him, "Ephphatha," that is, "Be opened."*

The first time I made the 2 noises that summon angles, I went into a vision. I saw a lighthouse. Its light was lite and it was rotating. The two main purposes of a lighthouse are to serve as a navigational aid and to warn boats of dangerous areas. It is like a traffic sign on the sea. I know the Lord was saying that these noises have the same function for angels as a Lighthouse does for boats.

Here are some Do's and Do not's for the intercessor.

CHAPTER THIRTEEN

7 Do's and Don'ts

1. The intercessor must understand and become acquainted with the Holy Spirit's authority. **Don't** be mistaken; this authority that pushes through you belongs to the Holy Spirit. You are only his vessel.

2. The intercessor must recognize and submit to authority. **Don't** get yourself off track by not being submitted to someone who knows the scriptures better than you. Make sure you are studying and checking against other established and recognized sources to be sure you are staying in line with scripture.

3. The intercessor needs to know the limits of their authority. **Don't** let the enemy deceive you about your authority. Remember, it's here on the earth. We don't go into the 2nd Heaven and start rebuking or commanding the fallen angels. We leave that up to the Lord.

4. The intercessor must learn the rules of engagement. **Don't** pray most of the Prayers found in books like "Prayers that rout demons: Prayers for defeating demons and overthrowing the power of darkness by John Eckhardt." Praying I bind, I loose, I break, I rebuke. I, I, I, I, I... Think about this, wouldn't it be a more powerful prayer if you replaced the word "I" with the word "Jesus"? Like this, I ask you, Jesus, to bind, loose, break, and rebuke...

5. The intercessor must seek a Holy life. **Don't** let the enemy convince you that the Lord does not call you to a life of continual sanctification. One of his strategies is to trick us into believing that it was all done at the cross. There is truth in that, but the devil is a liar. He uses scripture against us. Always remember there is MORE. There is a difference between our condition and our position. Read my husband's book "The Mysterious Keys to the New Testament. By Bruce Hines"

6. The intercessor must guard against impatience and not force God to act, but pray through for release. **Don't** go after your own will, but seek the Lords will His timing. The more you seek Him for His leading, the more He will share with you.

7. The intercessor must develop the character, purpose, and destiny of the movement for which they are praying. **Don't** get caught up in every "move" in the body of Christ. Keep your focus on what the Lord has you praying. STAND!! Which means, do not move and continue to agree with the Lord.

When someone becomes saved and in-filled with the Holy Spirit, the Authority that Jesus rules the heavens and earth by lives in them. The intercessor's job is to travail and stand in the gap until God's will comes to pass.

We know that the whole creation [of irrational creatures] has been moaning together in the pains

*of labor until now. And not only the creation, but
we ourselves too, who have and enjoy the firstfruits
of the [Holy] Spirit [a foretaste of the blissful things
to come] groan inwardly as we wait for the redemption of our bodies [from sensuality and the grave,
which will reveal] our adoption (our manifestation
as God's sons). For in [this] hope we were saved. But
hope [the object of] which is seen is not hope. For
how can one hope for what he already sees? Romans
8:22-24 Amplified Bible, Classic Edition (AMPC)*

An intercessory cry is "God, put an end to all the misery
of sin and end all the chaos on the Earth." The intercessor
must realize that travail, groaning, weeping, crying, and
roaring is a direct battle cry of authority.

It is the intercessor, in the deliverance, that pushes the
evil spirit out through travail. Other times, intercession
will create a powerful atmosphere for the church to do
deliverance to expel evil. Like a setup in volleyball where
the setter will setup for the spiker. Or the quarterback (intercessor) who reads the coverage and throws to the open
zone. It's the receiver's (the church, the body of Christ)
responsibility to see the coverage and run to the open
zone. That's intercession and spiritual warfare. The intercessor calls the play when they go to the line they scan the
defense (the kingdom of darkness) to see if the play needs
to be changed, at times they do! It is the church's job to
listen to the play or the audible, to see the open area and
run to it. That's travailing intercession working with the
body of Christ.

CORPORATE RENUNCIATION

Father God, in the name of Jesus, I ask you to forgive every sin I have committed, and every generational sin all the way back to Adam and the consequences of those sins. I renounce and break curses of those I or an ancestor have spoken evil of. I now forgive all who have sinned against me and past generations, that have brought hurt and destruction. I break every curse I have created and every generational curse my ancestors have created and their consequences, I ask for forgiveness Father God. Father, for every sin, transgression, iniquity, and the motives or intentions of the heart I ask for forgiveness and apply and accept the blood of Jesus to cleanse me and all generations walking the earth, and all future generations.

I renounce every form of sickness, disease and infirmity and the sins, transgressions, and iniquities that brought them into my life, even past and current generations. I repent for all heart issues and acts of rebellion that brought transgressions. I repent and break curse of all iniquity that brought perversity and crookedness into my bloodline. I apply the blood of Christ Jesus and accept His atoning sacrifice for my healing. I renounce the life behind every sickness, disease and infirmity and ask you God to drive it out.

I renounce all forms of the occult and/or other religions. I renounce divination and sorcery and the nine covenants of the occult. I renounce their ceremonies, rituals, blood rights, soul ties, all forms of covenants, spells, oaths, pledges, incantations, pacts, initiations, and memberships.

Every contract to the kingdom of darkness that I or my ancestors made, I now renounce and break them. I renounce my family name and bloodline that is on any or all alters and any or all offerings or dedications to the gods. Any and all fallen angels or demonic spirits worshipped, I renounce and break all covenants and the curses of worshiping fallen angels or demonic spirits. I renounce and break curses and covenants established through astral projection or evil spirit travel. I repent for my bloodline traveling on evil spiritual territory and memorial stones.

Father, if I or any ancestor gave their soul to the devil, I now renounce that and ask for forgiveness. I break that covenant, pact, blood right, pledge, and oath. I renounce the devil as god and confess that Jesus Christ is Lord to the Glory of God. I repent, break curses, and legal rights to all judgments in the spirit realm on all levels in God's courts.

Father, in the name of Jesus, I now ask You for every generational blessing due to me from the foundation of the world, and every anointing, ministry gift, character gift, talent, and gifting. I now speak this renunciation and prayer over every generation walking the earth and every future generation to come.

Father, right now, in the name of Jesus, I now command, in the name of Jesus and by the power of Jesus' blood, that every evil spirit, demon, infirmity and familiar spirit leave me by coming out of my soul and body and every part of me, all the generations walking the earth and all future generations, our DNA, chemical body make up and our blood lines.

I now thank and praise the Father of all creation for my salvation, healing, deliverance, and freedom from curses and poverty in Christ Jesus. I thank you Father for restoring me to my full inheritance in Christ Jesus.

REFERENCES

Amplified Bible (AMP)
Copyright © 2015 by The Lockman Foundation, La Habra, CA
90631

The Holy Bible, New King James Version
Copyright © 1982 by Thomas Nelson, Inc. Nelson, Thomas. Holy
Bible, New King James Version (NKJV) . Thomas Nelson. Kindle
Edition.

New American Standard Bible-NASB 1995 (Includes Translators'
Notes)
Copyright © 1960, 1962, 1963, 1968, 1971, 1972, 1973, 1975, 1977,
1995 by The Lockman Foundation A Corporation Not for Profit,
La Habra, California All Rights Reserved
The Lockman Foundation. New American Standard Bible-NASB
1995 (Includes Translators' Notes) (Kindle Locations 1410-1412).
The Lockman Foundation. Kindle Edition.

Logos Bible Software 8 - Copyright 1992-2019 Faithlife/Logos Bible
Software.
© 1998 by InterVarsity Christian Fellowship/ USA ® All rights
reserved. No part of this publication may be reproduced, stored in a
retrieval system or transmitted in any form or by any means, electron-
ic, mechanical, photocopying, recording or otherwise, without the
prior permission of InterVarsity Press.
Leland Ryken, James C. Wilhoit, Tremper Longman III. Dictionary
of Biblical Imagery (p. 1058). InterVarsity Press. Kindle Edition.

Barry, J. D., Mangum, D., Brown, D. R., Heiser, M. S., Custis, M.,
Ritzema, E., ... Bomar, D. (2012, 2016). Faithlife Study Bible (Jn
7:37). Bellingham, WA: Lexham Press.

Amplified Bible, Classic Edition (AMPC) Copyright © 1954, 1958,
1962, 1964, 1965, 1987 by The Lockman Foundation

Jacobs, H. E. (1915). Continual, Continually. In J. Orr, J. L. Nuelsen, E. Y. Mullins, & M. O. Evans (Eds.), The International Standard Bible Encyclopaedia (Vol. 1–5, p. 705). Chicago: The Howard-Severance Company.

https://www.nps.gov/apis/learn/kidsyouth/upload/LightCurrA.pdf

Volume 5: "Exploring Secrets of the Heavenly Realms: How fallen angels block healing. By Bruce Hines."

"Prayers that rout demons: Prayers for defeating demons and overthrowing the power of darkness by John Eckhardt."

"Christ's Last Order; Go Into All the World. By Derek Prince"

NOTES

Exploring Secrets of the Heavenly Realms

Vol. 1

AVAILABLE ON NOW AMAZON

EXPLORING SECRETS
OF THE
HEAVENLY REALMS

VOL. 2

AVAILABLE ON AMAZON

EXPLORING SECRETS
OF THE
HEAVENLY REALMS

VOL. 3

AVAILABLE ON AMAZON

Made in the USA
Coppell, TX
25 October 2019

10410052R00118